A Little Old Fashioned

Goes A Long Way!

Girl Talk Wisdom for Getting & Keeping
YOUR MAN

By Markita D. Collins

Imagine Media, LLC

A LITTLE OLD FASHIONED GOES A LONG WAY:
Girl Talk Wisdom for Getting and Keeping Your Man

Disclaimer

This book in no way intends to provide therapeutic information or intervention, but rather education and entertainment only. It does not replace the valid and often necessary work of a professional counselor. It is provided with the understanding that the author and publisher in no way are providing legal, financial or psychological advice. The reader, in so doing, agrees to take full responsibility for their well-being and safety in engaging with this material. The author and publisher specifically disclaim any liability for the use or application of the contents of this book.

ISBN 97809986970-0-0 (paperback)
Library of Congress Control Number: 2017902676

Printed in the United States of America.

Dedication

⎯⎯⎯⊃⊙⊂⎯⎯⎯

I dedicate this book to my Father God who is in Heaven and lives in my heart. Thank you!

I dedicate this book to my parents, Richard and Linda Faye. They are alive and well to witness this moment come to pass.

I dedicate this book to my husband Ali "Shaun" Collins. You are the reason why I believe "A little old fashioned goes a long way."

Acknowledgements

There are so many people I would like to acknowledge at this time; however I would be writing forever.

I want to thank every leader, pastor, teacher, evangelist, prophet, apostle, and intercessor who has made an impact in my life.

To all my ministry friends and family from all over the world, I love you all, and I'm honored you would see me as a sister and friend.

Thank you to every person that has sown into my life and has been a blessing to me and my family.

Thank you to every WIFE I've learned from, watched and gleaned from my whole life! To every WIFE who wants to do it "The Old Fashioned Way" and not lose who you are. I am praying for you. I pray this book inspires you.

Thank you to my business consultant Asha Tyson and your incredible team! I'll never forget the day you called me and said "Baby sis, it's time and I'm here to help you get there NOW!" That will always be the thing that I remember most. You said it and came through. Thank you for helping make my dream a sure reality!

This book may not have happened if these two men of God that I mention didn't speak over me at such a hard and crucial time: Pastor Albert Walker "Grandpa" and Prophet

Tony Kemp. I obeyed the Lord, and yes I finally wrote the book! Love you so much.

Cora "Brionne" Jakes Coleman. Thank you for your loyalty and friendship and being a real friend and covenant sister. I love you.

To my amazing Kita Team Shaun and Robyn! (lol) It's funny but so true that we are great together! Robyn...sis your part in my life was so timely. And for that I am grateful. Thank you for everything.

To my amazing supporters of *Girl Talk with Kita* and *Kita's Kompany* – I love y'all. You all have pushed me to be the best that I can on social media and beyond. Thanks for loving me and supporting everything I do. As your leader, advisor and instructor, I thank you from the bottom of my heart!

To the wonderful young people that call me "Auntie," TT, and Mom. You radical bunch ROCK! I stay in the know because of y'all! Thank you for trusting me with your hearts. Thank you for fighting for me and believing in me all the way. You matter to me.

Daddy and Mommy I am full of tears right now because I know you are able to read this part over and over again. You two have been together over 40 years and married 40. Daddy you have protected, provided, loved, fought for, and worked countless hours for your "girls." It's not often nowadays that fathers are even around to raise their children in one home to one wife. Thank you Daddy for being my number 1 guy! You taught me how to love people past their faults. You showed me how to be true to who I am...and to never let one monkey stop the show. You showed me that people will be people, and that doesn't change who we are. I love you for showing up for me time and time again. You were there during the worst times and greatest times. You never made me feel like I was too far not to come back home. I'll always be your "boogie" & Keet!

Mommy, Mommy, Mommy...you birthed me; you loved me; you spanked my butt and didn't play games with me! You felt every pain I ever endured. You taught me how to be a lady and never lose my self-worth. Even when you fought forces and were ridiculed, you found the strength to cover me in OIL and prayer! You required that I be a strong woman, but to always honor my father and husband. Thank you so much Mommy for being the rock you are to me!

To my Aunt Hattie and my Godfather Joe who is gone to be with the Lord...though you're not here, you were in my heart the whole time during this journey.

To my little sisters LaTrisha and Tracy: words can never describe our bond and strength as sisters. You two are amazing and I love you! Also my brother in-laws Garrett, Darreese and my nieces! We are truly an amazing family! No matter what we face we always come together. We laugh; we fight; we pray; we forgive; we love; we honor; and we protect and cherish one another. That's what FAMILY does!

Clarence the only thing that makes us not related is DNA! Thank you for being the greatest brother ever. We grew up in the same play pin and still closer than ever!

I want to acknowledge my whole entire family (Birdens, Kents, Cummingses, Littletons, Skipps, Collinses), Aunties, Uncles, Godmothers, Papas, sisters, brothers, cousins, all of you, both natural and spiritual.

Special love goes to all my godchildren – all 7 of you!

I want to thank God for the people I've met along the way that have stayed and those who are gone.

Last but not least, I must acknowledge my wonderful husband and beautiful children!

Josiah, Moriah, Mikaila, and Destin. Mommy loves you so very much. To my gift Aliana, you taught me how to be a great "Mother." Mimi loves you.

Shaun, what can I say, baby? I never knew that things would turn out this way with you and me. You are the reason it's easy to be a good wife. You're such an incredible husband. Being married to you makes me forget about the hurt that I endured in my past. You really helped me to let my guard down and stop being so angry. I'll never forget the day when you grabbed me and said "I'm not them! I won't hurt you!" That broke something in me and it never came back. You sir are so appreciated and my life has been far better since you found me. I thank God for you Shaun. I really do. I went from being broken to being healed. Now I'm whole because I've learned life's lessons. GOD is a good GOD and I will forever be grateful to Him for this moment right here and now. There's more to come...Thank you Jesus...There is much more to come!

~Markita D. Collins

Contents

King Says...

    I can recall walking into my 10th grade Biology class; it was day three of my first year at a new school. In walks this cute "chocolate girl" with a big smile and an even bigger air of boldness and confidence about her. I couldn't help but to notice how she commanded the attention of everybody in the room, but seemed to handle it with an "effortless grace." This intrigued me, as I lacked that degree of confidence and boldness: It was in that moment I made up my mind that she would be mine one day.

    Now, I don't know if it was love back then, but you can definitely say it was desire at first sight. Somehow I knew that everything I discerned in that first glance, were qualities I wanted and needed next to me (and did I mention she was cute?!).

    A few weeks after that, we were in class watching The Miracle of Life (which, as you can imagine, was an experience for a classroom full of fifteen-year-olds), and up until this point I had developed a crush on this "chocolate girl," but hadn't mustered up enough courage to even speak to her. So in typical Thunder Kat fashion, she taps me on the shoulder and says, "Hi! I'm Markita. What's your name?" "Shaun," I replied. Her next question set the foundation for the lady I would grow to know and love...she said, "Hi Shaun. That was an interesting movie. So what does it feel like when boys have sex?!" And thus the first Girl Talk was born.

When I think about life with my Wife, I liken it to driving a car. When you drive, you can't always just floor it and expect to get where you want to be safely; you have to learn when to accelerate and when to pump the brakes. There is a wisdom and a balance to driving, understanding the flow of traffic, while adhering to rules of the road.

The same is true for me as a husband to a strong wife, to arrive at our intended destination, there are times when I have to fall back and allow her to be who she is; there are times when I have to press and remind her of who I am!

Now, are there some "rules of engagement" when it comes to marriage and relationships? Yes. But I've learned to establish our own flow while keeping the "rules" in mind.

This "flow" is only established through communication, and I'm not talking about a one-sided, finger-pointing, victimized, monologue form of communication. I'm talking about a DIALOGUE, Hearing & Listening, Compromise, and Understanding a perspective outside of your own.

The most challenging part about my growth as a husband hasn't been her; it has been learning to humble myself, and letting go of an inherent desire to be the victor in every "battle" of my life.

George Herbert wrote, "Sometimes the best way to gain is to lose." It has been in those moments of "loss" or conceding that I have learned the most about myself and my spouse; those moments of revelation have consistently propelled us to our next level.

I have learned that His strength is made perfect in our weakness; when we embrace our shortcomings and allow God to work through our spouse, we become strong.

A good partner will enhance not hinder; they challenge you to stretch beyond your own expectations, they frustrate "in Love," and when all else fails, they pick up the slack and hold you down until you can get it right.

I have a spouse like this. She has taught me the difference between a woman and a lady; you're born a woman, biology and reproductive organs classify you as such; (most) men are hard wired to WANT a woman; but a lady, that's what we NEED!

Ladies aren't born, they are developed, through experiences, though trials, through maturation...A Lady personifies class, style, integrity: she knows when it's time to put her earrings on (and Stand), and when it's time to take them OFF (and Fight)!

I've heard it said that a man finds a wife. I would argue that he finds the raw materials for one. God never gives a man a finished product; He gives us the raw materials and charges us to CULTIVATE.

He doesn't give us the leather coat, He hides it in the cow. He doesn't give us a house, He hides the wood in the trees. He doesn't give us the Lady, He hides her in the woman. He doesn't give us the Wife, He hides her in the Lady.

I have been given the tremendous honor of cultivating one of God's greatest gifts; He has allowed me to pour trust, love and wisdom into her from the first day we spoke all those years ago. He has allowed me to be there through heart break, through joy, during the times when she was trying to rediscover who she was. He has allowed me to be there to help shape, mold and cultivate the woman, the lady and the wife I love today.

I am anointed to speak to the single woman, the married woman and the divorced woman. It matters not where you are in life or what your circumstances are. My message is not one for the faint of heart. This is real. There is not a relationship situation that I have not been part of. That's right. I can speak to it because I've been through it. And it took all of that for me to be able to say this. I am not a "wifey." I am not a "Booh." I am not a "Bae." I am a wife.

Maybe where you are right now is that you are single, and you want to be married. Or if you're married, you want it to be better. You need to know that your blessing is not going to come through familiar avenues. It's not going to come through what is known and comfortable to you. It's going to come through ways you can't see now. God's going to do it that way so that you know it's Him. Stop trying to make it come the way you want it to. Stop trying to force it or speed it up. This thing has to marinate in you. It has to take its time to get to you without you mucking up the works. You've got to surrender in this process and you've got to wait on it.

Wait. Wait without struggle. Wait without complaining. Wait without anger and frustration. Wait instead with your big girl pants on. Those assigned to you will come, but not through familiar hands. It's not going to come from people who know your "right now" story. They cannot hold the vision and the intention for your next story. Your job is to be in the receptive position to obtain the gift of blessing. Then as the blessing germinates in you, you must move to the birthing position to see it manifest. Your blessing is coming from a divine place of love and purpose. You will not miss it if you stay the course. You will surely see the Glory of the Lord for you in this if you be not weary.

This is the pathway.

Welcome to the journey.

My name is Markita Collins, formerly Markita D. Birden. I'm the eldest of three daughters of Richard and Linda Birden. Born and raised in Upstate New York, in my grandfather's church. Been singing since the age of four, and serving in ministry for just as long. I was educated in Catholic and public schools.

Growing up, all I knew was church and family. We were a family of love. There were always big dinners for Thanksgiving, Christmas and birthdays. Sunday dinners and card games after church was good living.

I saw only love between my parents. I saw them holding hands, hugging and kissing each other. They were really connected. While there was an electrifying unity, they sometimes disagreed, but even then there was a loving connection between them. No abuse, no disrespect. They communicated, and it was healthy. It's fair to say my parents were an example of a good marriage.

My father was a hard-working man who wanted the best for his girls. He wanted us to have top-notch and all things premium. My mother was a beautiful woman, always giving, serving and helping others. I remember when my mother didn't want to go to church any more. Even then my father made sure my sisters and I were at Sunday school every week at 9 a.m.

As a child, I wanted to be like my aunts. Lord knows they could sing! Singing to the glory of God until they sang down heaven was an absolute delight. Every time they bellowed, the Holy Ghost would move through the church, and people all around the sanctuary would be touched, healed and delivered as the Spirit of God moved among them. As I got older, I realized I had the same gift of song. I would sing and people would just fall out under the Holy Spirit.

As much as I had family that loved and adored me, I also had family members that were jealous and insecure, and didn't really love me like I thought they did. They talked about me, lied, gossiped and bullied me. It was a horrible experience that colored my perspectives and beliefs about life, people and me. For some reason, it was easier for me to believe the noisy, big-mouthed devil than it was to believe the still, small voice of the Spirit of God.

I was picked on at a young age because I was a braces-wearing, dark, chubby girl with a funky Jheri curl and a ring around my nose. I wanted desperately to fit in. I wanted somebody to accept me for who I was and just like me for being me.

My obsession to be accepted and approved of seemed to know no bounds. I made some bad decisions in my pre-teens because I wanted to be down with the "in" crowd. At the time, I didn't realize they didn't know who they were either and that's why they did the things they did. They were just like me – lost and looking for ways to fit in. Being bullied forced me to learn how to fight, and that's how I got noticed. I got all kinds of attention, adoration and respect when I finally stood up for myself.

I thank God for those childhood moments. It made me realize that no matter what people did to me, I still had to treat them with respect and let go of grudges. This prepared me for dating young men.

Skip to high school, where I fell in love. I was so young! When I fell, I gave my body. I wish I had waited, but I so desperately wanted to fit in. I was coming from a deep place of rejection. I again wanted to be down with this image of being chosen and made special by a man. What I now know is that it is demeaning to your soul and lasts longer than the few minutes spent exchanging your virtue. It wasn't worth it.

Being funny, talented and encouraging made me very popular in high school. I got along with faculty, staff and students. But then I started to notice that I couldn't get away with anything. I always got caught! I came to believe that it was the Lord's way of course-correcting me and showing me that I was special, gifted and anointed. At the time though, I was still dipping and leaning into wrongdoing.

After high school, I got married. He was in the military. He was strong and oh, so handsome. We got engaged, got married and moved to Georgia. I thought my life was perfect. It so wasn't.

He cheated on me during our relationship even before marriage. He gave me STDs. But he asked me to forgive him and I did...over and over again. I became depressed. I went from a size 12 to a 24. I was the epitome of sad. There was no joy, peace or satisfaction anywhere in my life. I was pretending to be happy when I really wasn't. I was supposed to be happy because he was an army man, a gentleman, a provider.

Although I was ready to be a wife, he wasn't ready to be a husband. When I look back now, I know he cared about me a great deal and he may have even loved me. But he didn't love me the way God wanted him to love me. And I suffered for that. I went through hell in that season. I got pregnant a couple of times, I was under so much stress, so much depression, that I miscarried. I asked God to show me what was going on I found proof that my husband was sleeping with other women. I was so hurt.

As Maya Angelou said, when somebody shows you who they are, believe them. He had shown me the truth about who he was; I just couldn't accept it.

Though I was faithful and did right by him, in 2003 he wanted out of the marriage. He told me this over an email! Can you believe it? What did I do to deserve this? I was faithful. I did right by you! Why couldn't you just love me the way that God expected you to love me? Why was that so hard?

We got divorced and it was the worst feeling in the world. He left me with nothing. All I had left were the car, my clothes, and a TV. I stayed in hotels, maxed out credit cards, stayed with friends who ended up getting tired of me. Finally I had to face the music and let my family know I had to come back home.

I packed my car with clothes and other belongings including "The Box" of stuff that he had given me. With a box of tissues on the passenger seat and gospel in the CD player, I drove 17 hours by myself with only enough money to get me home.

I was never suicidal, but I was really depressed, and I wanted to kill him for what he did to me. He destroyed my character. He destroyed me, or it sure felt like it. He mentally abused me. Emotionally abused me. And even physically put his hands on me. He completely disrespected me.

I was devastated. I was humiliated that this person had chosen me, told me he loved me, asked for my hand in marriage, then unceremoniously dropped me. I got angry at God and I didn't want no parts of nobody's church anymore. So I went to the world. I found what I thought was refuge in clubs and drinking and being with men. I thought, "I'm going to get him back for what he did to me." But I was hurting myself, not him, and the enemy knew it. I had to pull myself together and have a one-on-one with God and say, "Why did you allow me to go through this? I'm hurt. And I'm angry. I'm upset. I didn't deserve this."

After my time with the Lord, one of my aunts sat with me and prayed over me and counseled me and I had to really give up a lot. Eventually, I went to this church that operated in deliverance ministry. They especially seemed to reach women that were broken. I went there and I gave my all to this church.

Even with all of this support, I was still dealing with the ex-husband, allowing him to come in and out of my life. I would get my hopes up, just to be let down again. I had a soul tie to him. It was strong and it messed me up. I did not know how to let go.

A couple of years later, I ended up dating a man who I had known from my past. He told me he was divorced, when in fact he was still very much married and his wife was still very much in love with him. I know that feeling because I was cheated on. Why would I be with a man that's cheating on his wife? I wanted to let go, but I didn't know how.

He told me he was going to leave her. Told me that he had left her and was going to officially get a divorce so he and I could move on. I brought him into my world completely. I trusted him. And then he raped me.

I told my family, but nobody believed me, except my sister and my best friend, Shaun Collins. My sister had a way of pulling things out of me when I would shut down. She grabbed me and she said, "What's wrong with you, Kita? Something happened to you. Tell me what happened to you. Please. Why are you this way?" And I told her. I said, "He raped me. Now I'm pregnant and I don't know what to do." She said, "You gotta tell Mom and Dad."

So I told them. But they didn't believe me, which made me that much angrier. They said I was fornicating willingly, so it probably wasn't rape. Not even my own pastor believed me. Why would I lie about being raped? I didn't understand.

They wanted me to keep the baby, but I just couldn't. I couldn't imagine being with someone that had raped me. He raped me and he would have access to me and this child forever. I aborted the baby. I asked God to forgive me. And I asked the baby to forgive me. Now I had to forgive myself.

I didn't trust anybody, but I was still dating because there was this thing in me that felt like I needed a man. I just needed the company and the companionship of a man – any man. I was so blinded by what I thought love was and the need to be loved, that I settled for anything.

Then I became really close to my best friend, Shaun Collins. I had known Shaun since high school. Whenever I needed anything, he was always there for me. Little did I know, he had feelings for me, from way back in 1995! He had always been my friend – he was my best friend. One day, finally, Shaun told me how he really felt about me. And I told him how I felt about him. We were in love.

We did have a child out of wedlock. Josiah was our firstborn. I was surprised I even got pregnant again because every time I got pregnant before, I lost the babies. I think that was God's way of protecting me. He knew that I was supposed to have children with my husband. I know God has a sense of humor. On our honeymoon we conceived twins.

I brought Shaun to church and he gave his life to the Lord. God changed his heart. Saved Shaun. Filled Shaun with the Holy Spirit. And we've been rocking and rolling ever since.

Now, even in this relationship there has been drama. Family drama, baby-mama drama. We both had trust issues. We both were still broken and discouraged from our past relationships. We both were still unforgiving, but for some reason we still made it work.

I had to learn how to trust men again. I had to learn how to trust my gut again. I had to learn how to trust God again. I had to remember what my father and my mother instilled in me. I had to remember what the Word of the Lord said about me and that I deserved to be happy.

Shaun didn't have a lot of money like my exes did. He didn't have a lot of material things, but one thing he did have was my respect. He had a lot of love to give me. My husband is a hardworking, respectful man who treats me like a queen. When he looks at me I feel like I am the only woman in the room. He proved long ago that he is a provider, a protector, a supporter, a lover and a giver. An honorable man.

I remember after we got married I was still struggling with trust and anger from my past and Shaun said something to me that "triggered" a memory. It sent me almost seven years back and I went OFF! I was screaming and pacing back and forth, ready to fight. Shaun ran up on me and grabbed me by my arms and shook me one good time and said "Girl! Stop it, stop this right now! I am not them! I am not going to let you do this. I am not going to hurt you Kita! You have to trust me babe. I love you girl!"

At that moment something broke and I believed Shaun. I heard what he said and I fell in his arms and cried. I asked him to forgive me. I was very honest and told him, "I'm still healing; please be patient with me." I learned how to respect men again because of Shaun. Because of Shaun, I finally knew what it felt like to be adored, to be wanted, to be respected. Because of Shaun I didn't mind laying my pride to the side and submitting to him in a godly way. In an awesome way, Shaun proves every day that I made the right decision by letting go of my past and trusting him again. Together we learned to trust God again.

Our marriage has been tried by fire through the years. Shaun and I have endured money issues, sickness and health. Hurt by people in the church. Despised and just dragged by folks for no reason. I went through some of the hardest times with his child's mother. And God is still a loving God. He kept us through all of those transitions.

Five children later, including his oldest daughter, we moved from New York to Memphis, Tennessee, from Memphis, Tennessee to southern Pennsylvania. Ministering. Traveling the country. Singing.

I started a "Girl Talk with Kita" movement, which is a safe place for women who have gone through the things that I've gone through. I am intentionally being a testimony and a blessing. Now that I'm at this point in my life, I'm finally, finally saying, "I do deserve this life. And a little old fashioned does go a long way."

Forgiving people goes a long way. Being kind goes a long way. Loving people goes a long way. Being thankful goes a long way. Letting go of hurt goes a long way. Cooking goes a long way. Baking a cookie goes a long way. Giving him a glass of water goes a long way. Dressing appropriately and still being sexy, that goes a long way. Having an opinion but knowing when and where to share that opinion. It goes a long way.

I love Jesus for every trial I've gone through. I love God for every moment in my life and I praise Him every day for this journey that I'm on. I'm healed now. Healed from the abuse emotionally and physically. I am no longer broken. I am better for having gone through what I went through to get here. Now I am bold and victorious. I had to endure all of that to reach this place. I had to go through this to reach the girl who is rejected and don't need a man but who wants a man. I had to go through all of that to show that a woman can be strong and full of the Word and wisdom and still be tender with her man. I had to go through all of that to be every woman – single, married, divorced, rebellious, with married men, from a dark place, pregnant out of wedlock, promiscuous, rejected, hurt, abused, raped, couldn't get pregnant, aborted a child, stressed, alone, confused, prideful, and finally healed and happy. No woman can say to me, "You don't know what it's like." Yes I do, sister. I've been exactly where you are. And I can show you the way out. Listen to me and I'll get you from the dark, lonely, desperate place to the place of joy in the Lord in your loving husband's arms. Follow my lead. This work is anointed to bless you, to deliver you from hiding behind your own strength and fear.

The Lord has blessed me with a voice that emanates from my self-identity in Him. Your safe place is in God and in knowing who you are. By the end of this work, you will know that you are not alone. Your identity will shift to one of Conqueror. You will become secure in your identity as a woman with no residue of your past. This is possible for you, because He has done it for me.

———————⟡———————

I would be willing to bet that you have been told many times in your life who you are. We could start with simple definitions according to the roles you play or the relationships in your life. They might include: daughter, sister, friend, cousin, auntie, employee, community member, neighbor and likely many others. Or we could approach this conversation from a place of more personal discussion of the qualities you possess. You may be smart, friendly, outgoing, introverted, private, talkative, thoughtful, introspective, boisterous, and the like. But have you ever stopped to think about who God says you are? It might be worth more than a passing consideration, especially since He is our creator. Maybe it would be worthwhile to examine what He had in mind when He breathed life into us. After all, the purpose of the creation is established through the mind of the Creator.

The Word of God says that you are:

- Favored (Proverbs 3)
- Fearfully and wonderfully made (Psalm 139:14)
- Strong (Ephesians 6:10)
- Blessed (Deuteronomy 28:3-14)
- Wise (James 1:5)

Now I know this may be contrary to everything you've been told about yourself to this point. And I declare to you now, it is time to stop believing the lies and embrace the Truth. This may be the most challenging thing you face. It's so much easier to believe what we have been told by the world, even when there has been no compelling evidence to support it. Somebody decided something about us and we agreed. What?! What sense does that make? Somebody, probably with their own stuff, decided we were less than and we swallowed it and asked for more. Ladies and gentlemen, I put you on notice, right here and now it stops. No more will we allow the enemy to hoodwink and bamboozle us out of our true and rightful place in God.

Proverbs 18:22: "He who finds a wife finds a treasure and finds favor from the Lord." Think about it. Where is treasure found? In the hidden places. Treasure, that thing of great value, is hidden. It's not easily found. Wives in waiting, you need to know who you are and that you are treasure from the Lord. You are the fragrance of the house. You need to know you are valuable. You are like diamonds, pearls, rubies, sapphires and precious gems. Valuable. Start confirming it by telling yourself, "I am valuable."

When you allow people to tamper with you, lie to you or talk about you, your perceived value depreciates. Like a car, as soon as it leaves the lot, it loses its value. When you allow people to buy you and to treat you like an object, you lose your own value. You lose your value, daughter. You lose your value, queen. You lose your value, Woman of God. I declare it right now that you are favored. You are treasure. You are valuable.

When you don't allow who you are to sink into your spirit, you will believe what everyone else says about you and not what God says about you. You will let anyone fool with you and let them tell you you're not worthy of love and being cherished. It's about knowing who you are and not settling for the okie-dokie.

I need you to know you are not plastic. Not fake. Not glitter or crushed glass! You are not crushed glass! All sparkle and no substance or value. You're favored. A good thing. A treasure.

Wives – Proverbs 31: the virtuous woman
This is a beautiful scripture about the pricelessness of a godly woman. Here it is from the King James Version: Proverbs 31:10-31:

[10] Who can find a virtuous woman? For her price is far above rubies.

[11] The heart of her husband doth safely trust in her, so that he shall have no need of spoil.

[12] She will do him good and not evil all the days of her life.

[13] She seeketh wool, and flax, and worketh willingly with her hands.

14 She is like the merchants' ships; she bringeth her food from afar.

15 She riseth also while it is yet night, and giveth meat to her household, and a portion to her maidens.

16 She considereth a field, and buyeth it: with the fruit of her hands she planteth a vineyard.

17 She girdeth her loins with strength, and strengtheneth her arms.

18 She perceiveth that her merchandise is good: her candle goeth not out by night.

19 She layeth her hands to the spindle, and her hands hold the distaff.

20 She stretcheth out her hand to the poor; yea, she reacheth forth her hands to the needy.

21 She is not afraid of the snow for her household: for all her household are clothed with scarlet.

22 She maketh herself coverings of tapestry; her clothing is silk and purple.

23 Her husband is known in the gates, when he sitteth among the elders of the land.

24 She maketh fine linen, and selleth it; and delivereth girdles unto the merchant.

25 Strength and honour are her clothing; and she shall rejoice in time to come.

²⁶ She openeth her mouth with wisdom; and in her tongue is the law of kindness.

²⁷ She looketh well to the ways of her household, and eateth not the bread of idleness.

²⁸ Her children arise up, and call her blessed; her husband also, and he praiseth her.

²⁹ Many daughters have done virtuously, but thou excellest them all.

³⁰ Favour is deceitful, and beauty is vain: but a woman that feareth the LORD, she shall be praised.

³¹ Give her of the fruit of her hands; and let her own works praise her in the gates.

Look at this woman! She is phenomenal! She knows her business. She is a help to her husband. Her husband has full confidence in her. Look at how he regards her. She is trustworthy and has proven herself so. She is not sitting around idle. She's not a nagger. She doesn't appear to have time to nag. She's taking care of everyone including the poor. She brings great ideas. She's not lazy, she's industrious. She's creative and a force to be reckoned with in the marketplace. Where did we get the idea that a stay-at-home mom can just sit on her rear-end all day or just go shopping?

A virtuous woman has money. She's not waiting on her husband to do everything. She's got skills. She can take care of herself and her family if need be. If anything ever happened to my husband, I could get some flour, and sugar and do something to make money. I can flip Kita's Kookies and Treats into a full-time gig and still get the bills paid and the living expenses handled.

The Virtuous Woman out of her earnings, she plants a vineyard. She is a business woman. She takes care of the business of her family. And notice that it says, "Out of her earnings, she plants a vineyard." Out of her earnings. She has more than one business. This woman has multiple streams of concurrent income that she uses to increase her businesses. She's not out spending every extra dime that comes in on Gucci and Louis, shoes, purses and furs. She's putting the money back into the businesses. Taking the earnings from one to increase another. That's wisdom in business.

Now I want to be clear because I hear you saying to yourself, "I'm not good at business. I can't do all of that." What I know is whether or not you are good in business, there is something you do well. There is something at which you excel. Do it. As long as it is legal and morally appropriate, do it. Do it to the very best of your ability and God will bless the labor of your hands. Because of your obedience, the Lord will open the heavens, the storehouse of His bounty, to send rain on your land in season, and to bless all the work of your hands (Deuteronomy 28:12).

Okay, hear me…especially you single ladies…you think that when you get married you have to lose your voice and opinion. Stop choosing with your flesh and start choosing with your faith. You only run into that problem when you chose a man who's insecure and who is not confident in you. That's why it's important for the man to find you. Look again at the regard the husband has for the virtuous woman. Verse 28 says, "Her children arise up, and call her blessed; her husband also, and he praiseth her." He's praising her! Not dogging her out, not abusing her, not threatened by her skills and accomplishments. He's praising her! That is significant in regards to their relationship and consideration of one another. Does that sound like a woman whose husband wants her to keep quiet? Or does he appear to value her opinion and input? When you marry the one that God has for you…he will honor and respect your opinion. Marriage brings you into agreement with your husband. The necessary, Godly family structure is this – God first, for everyone, husband/wife second, then children, then everybody else. For the marriage to work and be successful, God has to be at the center.

Another thing I want to bring to your attention is that the marriage has to be between two adults. By that I mean, you didn't marry your daddy and he didn't marry his mama. You came together as adults making adult decisions and doing adult things.

Eve was a full grown woman when she was created. We don't know how long Adam was asleep. She was presented to Adam as a full grown woman. Some of you are presenting yourselves to men as toddlers because you don't know who you are. You're looking for your man to be your daddy. He's not!

Eve walked with God too. She spent time with the Lord. Are you? Do you spend more time with social media than you do with God? Are you spending more time with dating sites trying to make it work yourself? A lot of men are especially afraid of African American women. We haven't been taught submission without being walked all over. Too many bitter, angry women are sharing false information about men and relationships. They are speaking their experiences as truth. When in truth they are only sharing their painful experiences. No one would dare minimize their pain. It is real for them. However, it is not Truth with a capital "T." Only God's Truth will stand. And whatever you got from the world as an interpretation of your situation needs to stay in the world. It has no place in your marriage or your relationship. You cannot allow someone else's bitterness and pain to inform your relationship decisions.

There are some singles who are anointed to speak and teach on marriage. Paul wrote almost a third of the New Testament and he was single. Jesus was single and taught on marriage. I'm not disregarding them. But if you are listening to people who are convincing you not to get married, you need to change the people you are listening to.

When you are with the right man, you don't want nobody else. You need to allow God to change your concept about what a wife is. I'm excited when I look at my husband. I'm happy. I'm full of joy. It doesn't stop men from being attracted to me. Of course they're attracted to me and my joy. Even more so because I'm happy. They are seeking and want to know that happiness as well.

And stop letting people get into your marriage where they don't belong. No one can talk about my husband. Not even my mom. I don't care what he's done. That's my husband. Keep your mouth off of him. And ladies, what happens in your house between you and your husband should stay in your house. No argument should be shared. It only taints your family's or friends' opinions of him. So when you fall back in love with him, they're still thinking about the argument. And hear me well…stop sharing how great he is in bed with your best friends, single or married. That's how mess starts and suspicions get cast. Then you start thinking everybody wants your man. Keep that sacred place between you and your husband where it belongs.

Now you're going to teach people how to treat you and your spouse in your presence. It comes from knowing who you are and loving yourself. I am a strong woman and I have to have a man that can appreciate that. I need a man who can be a cover for me and where I can be soft and tender without being run over. God knew that when he gave me my husband.

Some of you saw your mamas get beat. And some of you saw your aunties get beat. So now you gotta prove to the world that you're not that girl. That you ain't goin' down like that. You're so strong you missed it! You missed the one God prepared for you when you ran over him with your attitude and your bravado. You missed it when you dismissed that quiet, confident soul that approached you. You missed it when you had to prove your strength and importance and couldn't be still long enough for him to touch you. 'Cause you still don't know who you are.

Stop being bitter because no one proposed this year. Maybe it's not your year. Stop being stuck. Maybe you gotta get your passport and go somewhere you can be found. Stop recycling the same dudes in your little location. See the world. Travel. Stop looking at the prom picture feeling some kind of way about your high school prom date.

Do you know who you are?

My declaration for you:

- You are fearfully and wonderfully made
- You are a woman of integrity
- You are a treasure in an earthen vessel

Whether light skinned, dark skinned, natural hair, no hair, Brazilian hair that you bought to sew in or glue in, big eyes, slanted eyes, eye brows, no eye brows, short, tall, skinny, fluffy, flat booty, round booty, no chest, big chest, you are still worthy of a man to find you and be committed to you.

But you have to know who you are. Stop letting TV, these waist trainers, these butt lifters, these lip injections, these popular personalities fool you into thinking you have to be them to be desired. They are not living your life, you are. They are not in your circumstance or situation, you are. You are doing the best you can with what you have and who you are. This is your journey, not theirs.

Know who you are in God. Know who God is through you, and nothing shall be impossible unto you. In a time of stillness and quiet contemplation, ask God to show you the way He sees you. You might be amazed at the images He shares. Images of you as royalty having dominion and power. Images of you as precious and chosen. Images of you as special. Images of you as a virtuous woman. This is who you are. Nothing less.

I am married. I am not a mistress. I am not with anyone else. I am not dating other men. I don't want anyone else. I am secure in my identity as a woman and as a wife.

According to urbandictionary.com, the "side-chick" is the other woman, also known as the mistress; a diva that is either a male's wife or a girlfriend who has relations with the male while he is in another relationship; not even the girlfriend. That's the world. Its definition relates to extra-relationships, outside of the primary couple. God with His infinite wisdom takes it bit further.

How many of us have been the side-chick, even to our spouse or fiancé? How many of us are second to our husband's job, career, business, step-children, children, in-laws, mamas, daddies, baby-mamas, the church!

How many of us have become the other woman? How many of us have come home faithfully, done what we were supposed to do as wives and still end up as the side-chick? The side-chick doesn't get the accolades of a wife, fiancée or girlfriend. She's just a stand-by. How many of us have stood by being married or in a relationship but feeling single?

Today is the day of freedom and revelation. God wants to heal you of that. Do you know why? Because some of us have made God our side-chick. Picture it. You come to God only when you want Him. Only when you need something. You have no allegiance to God. You have no compassion for God. You don't even respect Him. But you want God when you're in a bad place or you need Him to fix something. Side-chicks are fixers and the antidote to an addiction. We have put God in the category of a side-chick. I don't want to do God like that anymore. I want Him to be the lover of my soul. I want God to know that "When I wake up in the morning, I want to make You smile. When I wake up in the morning I don't want to sound foreign to You. When You hear my voice I'm not just randomly dialing Your number because no one else is available." That's what side-chicks are. When the girlfriend isn't available, when the wife isn't available, the side-chick is always available. The side-chick drops everything to come see about someone that doesn't even belong to her. The side-chick is borderline prostitute, a high-priced geisha. A side-chick is the woman that will never get the husband. But again how many of us have been the side-chick in the Spirit? Where we are legally bound to somebody or we are getting ready to walk down the aisle with somebody and we're competing with other things in the way. When are you gonna come to the realization that you don't have to be the side-chick? Even if you are sleeping with someone or being with someone who doesn't belong to you, God has so much more.

I have so many women come to me and say, "I get it Markita. But what you need to understand, Woman of God, is that you lay next to triceps and biceps every night. You have a husband that loves you and you have a family and this and that." And I tell them I know how they feel. I've been there, done that. I was in love with a man that didn't belong to me. I didn't know that he had a wife, that he had a child. But because of flesh and because of lust and because of being out of the will of God, my emotions got all wrapped up and my soul got tangled up in that. I didn't know how to get out of it. I had to cry out to God to get me out of that. I didn't want to be the side-chick. I'm not the wife. I'm not the girlfriend. I'm the other woman. I'm the adulterous woman. I said, "God, I gotta get outta this. I gotta change the way I think. I gotta pack up and move. I gotta get in the car and drive. I do not deserve to be in this mess. I gotta get outta here. 'Cause I'm more than the other woman. I'm more than the side-chick."

So what do you do? First you've got to remember who you are. You are favored. It's your name and a lot of you don't even know what your real name is. You think your name is Doretha. You think your name is Jackie. Do you really think your name is Robin? Do you really think your name is Helen? No my queens, my darlin's, my princesses, my sisters. Your name is "Favored." When you realize favored is treasured, you will hold yourselves up. You will esteem yourselves in a different way. TV reality shows and what you see on social media is not our reality when we're in God. And no, it is not God's intention for you to be bitter and upset and mad because for some reason nobody has found you yet. He can't find you because you're with somebody else.

Or your husband can't find you because you've allowed yourself to be second to everything else. Tell that man, tell that husband of yours to listen...communicate. This is my next point: communicate with grace and with wisdom and passion. "I love you; I'm in love with you, but listen, we got to spend time together because I feel like I'm in competition with your computer. We gotta hold hands and I need you to hold me and cuddle me and go with me for a walk. I need that because I feel like every time your mother calls, you drop everything for her but you won't drop everything for me."

"I need you. I need you to be there for me like you're there for the kids. Like you're there for the pastor." So you've got to convey that with passion and with humility. "Listen, I got to get this off of me. I can't be the other woman. I can't be the wife that you treat like the side-chick."

You have to be careful, Wife, that you are not so humble that he forgets and starts to take you for granted. Sometimes you gotta remind your husband, "Honey, I'm over here." Because he's so relieved that you're not a nagger. He's so relieved that you don't bug him about everything. He's so relieved that he can trust you to handle those kids that you did not birth for him. He's so relieved that he doesn't have to worry about you spending all the money. He's so relieved that you're not all over him. Sometimes you get lost in the "Oh that's my girl. She's good over there. I don't gotta worry about her." Then you'll internalize that and it will become hidden rejection. Then it will become a fit that will rise up and you'll start noticing how he drops everything for everybody when you feel like he won't drop anything for you. And unless it's addressed in a healthy way between you, it festers and turns into resentment and unresolved anger.

You are not the side-chick and I'm telling you what to do to get yourself back in order. Use wisdom. This is not the time to confront him with anger and rejection. Build him up with appreciation and admiration. Assume the best about him and his choices where you are concerned. Avoid believing the worst. Could it be that he is not intentionally overlooking you, forgetting about you? Could it be that you are the only stability in his life right now and he is actually grateful that you are not as needy as the others? Shower him with praise and reminders that you're still on his side. "Honey, I love you. You're so good to me. You're so kind to me. I appreciate you. Baby, you rock. You're not alone. I got your back. You're not by yourself. You're not holding everything down on your own. I won't bother you. But I do need a little hug and a little loving every once in a while. I need you to make love to me, hold me, kiss me on the forehead once in a while. I need that from you. Without me telling you. I want you to treat me how you treated me when you first got me. Remember when you first got me? You wrote me letters and notes and held my hand and you opened the door for me. You courted me. I still need that." You need to let him know how that made you feel. "I remember when you used to do that and it made me feel so good." So you won't be the side-chick and then you resent him. Because you see how eager he is to do for everyone else while you feel like second fiddle.

And to my single ladies who desire to be a wife, here are some hints and tips for you when your husband does find you. When the man does find you, you will know what to say and what to do. What you don't want to say is, "Listen, we're getting married so you tell yo mama n 'em that they better get it in line. I'm your wife, not them." No. If he's a man of God and he loves the Lord, he understands order. Sometimes you have to remind him of the order. If you have to go into the relationship schooling the man then you got a boy, not a man. But he who findeth a wife findeth a good thing and receives favor from the Lord. God didn't call you to be dealing with a boy that you have to teach and instruct. Adam was a full grown man. Eve was a full grown woman.

Who are you with? Are you with somebody that you have to teach and school? Are you with somebody that you gotta constantly remind, "Thus sayeth the Lord?" Did he find you or did you find him? Are you having to teach him how to be a man? Being a man is not limited to providing and covering. I want an entire man.

It's too late in the day to try to figure out if you're with a boy or a man. It's too late in the day to be side-chick to some man who doesn't realize who you are. So who are we letting pick us up? Have we become projects? Have we become the answer? Are we healing the system? Are we getting to the root of some stuff? Because most often side-chicks come because there is something that the wife is not fulfilling. It's not fair. And it's not right. Most often the side-chick is doing something that the wife or the fiancée is not doing. Are we affirming our men enough? Are we celebrating our men enough? Are we pushing our men the right way? Are we pulling them to an expected end? Are we pulling them up to the vision? Are we reminding them of the vision? Can we remind them of the vision when they kinda fall off? Are we helping them along the way? Or are we the kind of women that would push our men into the arms of something, or someone, that feels safe though it is very dangerous?

Most side-chicks, unless they are really, really bold, don't want to be side-chicks. But she settles because she knows, "I'm giving him something that his wife isn't giving him." That's what she thinks in her mind. But she's delusional. She's thinking, "I'm giving him something that he can't get from them so he has to get it from me. So I'm okay being the other woman because then I don't have to obligate myself." Side-chick, you need to get healed, and you need to get delivered. Leave people alone.

At the end of the day, God is still God. And He will deal with that man at the appointed time. The wife will deal with the husband. Wives you never deal with the side-chick. Hear me…wives never deal with the side-chick. You don't come down from the tower, Rapunzel. You stay up there until it's time to come down. You don't deal with people who are trying to attack your marriage. You pray and you believe God. You deal with him, you don't deal with her.

See, we weren't taught right. We were taught to fight the girl. And the guy just sits there like, "What's going on?" So girls, you both have been duped again. He did it. Why are you trying to fight another woman when she was duped too? She should have known better, but she was just messed up in her mind. I've been there. Telling myself this is all that I deserve and didn't know how to come up out of it, until the Lord dealt with me.

You don't wanna be nobody's wifey. Pray this prayer
with me:

Father, in the name of Jesus, I praise you and thank you
for who you are and what you've done in my life and in
our lives. I pray that you bless and keep covered, God,
these women and all that is taught and that is being
received. I declare and decree in the name of Jesus that
no weapon that is formed against these women and
anyone they are connected to shall prosper. Thank you
Lord for teaching us how to do things the Wifely Way.
Thank you, God, for giving us courage and wisdom,
knowledge and understanding on how to go to the next
level in our marriage. And if we're not married, how to
become ladies in waiting and wives. If we're going
through divorce, how to heal and recover. Father, I
thank you that you're healing us from the inside out. I
thank you that you are truly the lover of our souls and
there is no good thing that you will keep from us if we
walk uprightly before you. Father, I thank you for every
reader that represents favor. I thank you for every
reader that represents the kingdom of God. Lord, I
thank you for every woman that is going to the next
level in you because she trusts the word of this Woman

of God. And I believe with all my heart that you are still Lord. In Jesus' name, amen.

God never wanted you to be a "wifey." He wanted you to be a wife. So who are you gleaning from? Who taught you how to be a wife? What are some of the examples you have and the lessons that you've learned? Are you reading the Word of God? Are you studying people? Do you find yourself looking at TV? Did you learn from the Cosby Show or your favorite comedy show? What was your idea of marriage? What is your idea of being a wifey? Do you think it is the same thing as being a wife? Do you think that God wants you to waste years and years of your life and time waiting on somebody to finally realize who you are and choose to marry you? Are you limiting yourself to greater possibilities? Are you giving your body up to someone who doesn't belong to you, who keeps promising that he will marry you? Do you have the stamina to stand and wait? Or are you too afraid to walk away? Are you in a relationship that you know is not healthy and you know God wants you to leave that relationship but you don't know what else to do? So instead of being a wife, you settled for being a wifey. What are some of the things you're doing? How are you preparing yourself? What are you saying to yourself?

At this point in the game, what we know is that we have value and worth. We also know that God never made us the side-chick. We are going to learn now that being a wifey, a live-in girlfriend, or someone waiting on him to make up his mind is also not what God intended. Are you willing to let it all go and wait for someone that God wants you to be with, or are you going to settle because you're afraid to release and let go?

Statistics say that nowadays most marriages last from three to eight years. Statistics say that usually people whose relationships end in divorce get married two to three years later. Statistics also say that the longer you date, the longer your marriage. These are the world's systems. I believe that as a Woman of God, God has a system for us. And we need to do things the way God wants us to do them.

If we learn the principles of what dating, courting, engagement and marriage are, we would not go through this revolving door of marriage. If we stop confusing dating and engagement, and courting and marriage, we would not be in these situations where we are constantly turning over relationships. Stop giving away your territory to people who shouldn't have free reign in your life. "Here's the key to my house. Here's the key to my car. Come move with me. Come stay with me."

Do you know the difference between dating, courting, engagement and marriage? And for the wives reading this, you need to know that there are still things you need to learn as a wife. Have you been tricked into thinking that your way is the greatest way? Are you up for learning how to change the way you perceive things? Are you up for the challenge of asking God to show you where you might have stepped off the track? Are you willing to hear how to strengthen your marriage, and how to be more of an aid to your marriage instead of a hindrance? Do you believe you're doing all the things that you're supposed to do in your marriage?

Being a wifey is a disrespect to you. I know and understand that it is a trendy word and it sounds real cute. I'm not coming for anyone or knocking what others may think a "wifey" is, but there's nothing cute about being a "wifey"! Wifeys never become the wives. Wifeys do everything the wife does but she does not get the ring. She doesn't get the claim. She doesn't get to say, "I am his wife." She doesn't get to have his last name. She doesn't get to have the things legally that a wife does. She doesn't get to walk around proudly and declare that she is his beloved, that she is his good thing. She does not have the luxury of any of that. All she can say is that "We live together and it works out for us." In her mind she has accepted that "This is all that I can get." She has decided that this is the only way to be with someone and has become okay with it. In reality, the wifey is never okay with it. She's just too scared to detach and let go of whatever connection she thinks she has. So she allows the disrespect to pile on and lets the years go by. Then there are children. They may be able to have the father's last name but she'll never have it. Or ten or twelve years later he decides to marry her. There are too many people telling the wifey not to mess up a good thing…like this man who refuses to marry her is such a prize. No one will tell her that she deserves better than that. She deserves to be respected.

Maybe the problem is that he doesn't know how to be a husband. Maybe he never had the role models he needed to know how to respect you. Maybe he wasn't taught properly, not that it is your job to teach him. Maybe he doesn't know how to court you, how to love you, how to not put you last. Maybe he didn't know that he had to come in with vision. Maybe he didn't know that he had to make a decision to choose you and leave everybody else alone and move forward versus hanging on to his past of whatever it was he saw. Maybe he didn't have a male figure telling him how to treat a woman and how to be a man. What you do for a lady. Maybe he just plain didn't know.

But ladies, even if he doesn't know, you should. You should know the difference between being a wifey, a "Booh" and a "Bae," and a wife. We have totally changed the structure of God's kingdom. We are okay with living with somebody first, having their babies, and then getting engaged then getting married. That is so backwards! We are so okay with having someone live with us for three and four years, sleep with them, cohabitate with them, do everything together and then maybe we'll get married or maybe we won't. We have become so comfortable with sin that when somebody is doing it right, we consider it strange. We've gotten so used to dysfunction that we think it's normal.

Check this out. To qualify for a gastric by-pass surgery, you have to be a certain weight. In order to get the surgery to help you lose weight you must weigh a certain weight. The doctors have made it so desirous to have this surgery, that people are gorging themselves in order to gain the weight to get the surgery to lose the weight. That's crazy. That's dysfunction. Why does that make sense? Sure, sometimes people need extreme help to lose weight, but the rest of us just need to fall back to the basics that still work and are healthy. Exercise, eat less sugar and carbs, eat more fiber and green vegetables, drink water and lots of it.

That same theory goes for relationships. Stop doing what everybody else is doing just because it's become the common way of doing things. Stop putting everything in your name – cable, phone, car payment, the house or apartment, the utilities, you're buying all the groceries, letting him sleep in your bed. He helps "when he can." You're having his babies and hoping he's going to marry you some day. Hoping someday he'll see your worth and choose you above all others. How can he see it if you don't?

God never wanted that for you. He does not want you to be around someone who is just a baby-layer and a user. Someone who is just there to make you feel good and keep you company. When you are a wifey, he can just come and go as he pleases. There's no real commitment. Why would you believe or expect that God would not want you to be married? Why do you believe you have to help God by living out of order, just to have a man? You don't know if he's going to choose you or not. I have worked with women who were with a man many years without being married. He fell out of love with her, left and was married within the next year. Do you know how devastating that is for a woman? "You spent all that time with me when you didn't have nothin', living off of my income and my resources. When you didn't have anything, I was your everything." Don't limit yourself to being that man's wifey. It's a disrespect to who you really are. And if you have been through divorce, you don't have to rush into marriage. You need to heal. Heal and take your time. It does not mean that you'll never be married again.

I was divorced and now I'm married to an amazing man. I'm happier than I ever imagined possible. When God does a thing, He does it so well. There are times I literally forget about what I've endured. And the only reason that I discuss what I've been through is to help someone else with my testimony. I share to help bring someone else out of their dark places. Otherwise I wouldn't have anything to complain about. My husband is good to me. He was sent by God to find me. He knew I wasn't his wifey. He knew I wasn't his "Bae." He knew I wasn't just his honey. He knew I was his wife, his good thing.

Those of you who are married have an assignment. You are to help your husband meet the goal, manifest the vision, help keep him on task, bring things to his remembrance. You've got to make sure this man is focused. Sure, you want to be attractive to him. You want to stay desirable for him. But your responsibility to your husband goes further than that. You have to be an aide to him, to remind him of the call on his life.

You don't do all of that for your boyfriend or your significant other. Why should you? What's the commitment? Reserve that for your husband. Care about your boyfriend all day long, but don't be wifey. Why should he buy the cow when he can get the milk for free? Think about it. Why should he marry you when you are already giving him everything that a wife would give him? I am not saying that you play the "I don't think so because I'm not your wife," games. You should never be petty. But you've been with someone for some three or four or five or ten or twenty or thirty years, it's past time for a decision to be made. It's time for holy matrimony to take place. And let me be clear, there are some who are married and it isn't holy. It was not created by God. God never told them to get married to that person. So those marriages were not ordained by God. He honors them because He honors covenant, whether He was in it or not. When He sees marriage He sees covenant.

You don't have time to play house. You don't have time to test the waters to see what it's like to live with him. To be honest we can't cohabitate with the opposite sex, unless it's a relative. The majority of us would sleep with them. I have a cousin who's been engaged for the last thousand years. She and her fiancé live in a two-bedroom apartment together. All the while she's telling us they're waiting to get married and he sleeps in his room and she sleeps in her room. Huh. Well guess who's pregnant? We just can't do it y'all.

Why are we settling? Do you know people are teaching classes on how to be a wifey? They're actually teaching people how to stay in bondage. They're teaching people that God doesn't have to design our relationship; we can do it ourselves. They're teaching people how to accept that they may never get his name.

The message is that I have his body, his children and his "respect" and I'm happy with that. I know people in their fifties, sixties and seventies who are just now getting married to their "baby-daddy." They lived together twenty and thirty years. The kids are in college and they are just getting married. Why didn't anyone tell these ladies they should be married?

They should not just accept that they're living together and it works. He does his thing, she does her thing. What about medical insurance? What about bankruptcy? What about legacy? What about LIFE?!

God will give you a way and a strategy to handle all of that. Do you think we're talking about a God that can't fix your credit? That can't get you out of bankruptcy? Do you think we're talking about a God that can't help you out of legal situations? Do you think we're talking about a God that can't work it out for you? Don't you believe the God of the Bible you read? Don't you believe the God that you pray to that makes this stuff right?

Don't ever, EVER settle for being somebody's wifey when God said your name is Favor. How can your name be Favor if he doesn't marry you? How can your name be Favor if he doesn't find you and choose you for the long haul? You deserve it. Why would you ever make it okay in your mind, "Well this is what it is and I'm okay with it." You should not be okay with that. Something ought to be stirring up in you right now telling you that you deserve more than that.

This is no shade to men because I believe this generation has not been taught. I'm talking about this generation, this thirty-five and under crew. They are different. They don't understand the biblical principles. It has order and it has structure and there is nothing corny about doing it God's way. You're blessed when you do it God's way. You're blessed when you do what God says. You shouldn't want to be a statistic. You shouldn't want to be the one who stays married for two years after living together for twenty. Do you know that God is obligated to bless you when you do it His way? He's obligated to bless you.

You can't do it the world's way and expect to be blessed. The world will tell you that it's okay to masturbate and touch yourself. God says, "That is not Me, I'm not in that." The world says it's healthy. The world says you're releasing toxins and pheromones. What about what God says? He wants your bed to be pure. You have to believe the Word of God. His methods are always right.

You do not deserve to be chosen last. You do not deserve to be waiting for someone to realize who you are and waiting for someone to pick you and to see your value. You deserve more than holding him down and being his ride or die chick. You deserve to have that man's last name. You deserve to have him honor you, protect you and cover you the right way. And if he can't do that then you've got no business with him in the first place.

The only reason you are with a man that isn't doing all of that is because you're scared, lonely and horny. Scared of being alone. Your body is craving. And if he walks away, you're asking yourself, "What will I do? I have these kids.

What will I do? Am I going to work another job? Am I going to have to get government assistance? Am I going to have to move back in with my parents?" You cannot allow fear to keep you so captive that you don't believe God to turn it around for you.

So I prophesy to you right now: The spirit of fear is broken off of your life right now. Make a decision. I prophesy that God gives you wisdom, courage to stand, strength to endure. Some of you will be rejected. You'll have to make some decisions and it's gonna hurt your feelings. And you're not going to understand why you're going through what you're going through. But on the other side of this I decree and declare that it will make sense to you. I decree and declare that your later will be greater than your now. I decree and declare in the name of Jesus, that you will not be held captive by being limited in your marital status. That you will not be bounced around. That you will not feel the drop. That you will not be embarrassed. That you will not be ashamed to walk away. But that you will have the poise of a woman. You will have poise and grace and be dignified. You will not accept anything less because you are a wife. You are nobody's wifey, you're nobody's sex toy. Nobody's play thing. Nobody's guessing game…do I want you or not? Nobody's sleeping-over buddy. Nobody's baby-layer. Nobody's baby-mama. You're a wife. And as a wife, I speak into your life, you will do things the wifely way. Honor that man, you will cover that man in prayer, you will honor him as your husband. It is not hard for you to shut your mouth and listen. You will trust your husband. It is not hard to come into agreement with him. I declare that you have the strength to endure. I believe God is giving you the grace and the patience to work this stuff out. Because He never intended you to be a wifey.

I think to myself when I see these ladies who have given their lives away and settled for being the wifey how tragic it is that she doesn't know who she is. If she did she would never put up with that nonsense. She would never settle for that. You have to know the power you have as a wife. You have to know the influence you have. You have to know how the enemy hates you and wants you to be depressed and dealing with low self-esteem. He wants you to think you're too bossy, too arrogant. He wants you to think there is something wrong with you. He wants you to think you'll never get out of the ghetto. He wants you to think there is no hope for you. As a man thinketh so is he. If you are not thinking on the things of God then you're focused on the things of the world. God is saying you're a wife but you keep hearing wifey. God keeps saying your name is Favor and you keep hearing "not good enough." You are a woman of God. You are a wife.

I know where your head went when I said that. We can go with a lot of angles for this. Let's just make this very clear. You will miss the God-intended opportunity to be with an amazing man of God by doing the following things.

- Comparing him to your past
- Comparing him to other men that have money or a lack thereof
- Comparing his size
- Comparing ring sizes
- And comparing your life to somebody else's life

Let me say this: What God has for you ladies is definitely for you. Specifically for you. Meaning that when God created you, He knew specifically who He wanted you to be with. A lot of times we fall out of the will of God. We fall out of the perfect will of God and we go into the permissive realm. We start trying to make things happen spending time with people we have no business dealing with.

Now let me tell you this: dating is fine. There's nothing wrong with dating. Dating is just an activity. It's like a sport. We're collecting data. It's the "introduction stage." Dating is not me falling in love and being intimate. You want to get to know me and I want to get to know you. A problem arises when we get dating confused with courting and engagement and marriage. We start sleeping with people that God never intended us to have a relationship with, ever. We start making decisions with our flesh, which is weak.

Think of all the men you've been with. Hopefully there have not been many. But just think of them. Think of all the people you let come into your life, come into your spirit, come into your space and literally come inside of you. God never intended that.

Now, because we have information we were never intended to have, we compare sizes of men. Many times outside of the will of God, we begin to compare one to another. He's not big enough. His car isn't big enough. His bank isn't big enough. His degrees aren't big enough. His penis isn't big enough. His tongue, his hands, his height, his weight, his feet, his nothing is big enough.

Meanwhile, God is saying He has the one for you. Remember your name is Favor. He didn't create you to be a tester. He didn't call you to figure this out. He doesn't require that of us. He didn't intend for you to experiment to find the answer. He created you to be the hidden treasure. How are you hidden if you are out trying to find him yourself? Seriously, we need to stop playing God in this. He doesn't need our help. He is God and God alone.

To the marrieds…you have to get the man out of your head and spirit. Unless you've been delivered and set free from your past, you are literally laying down with your husband comparing him to the men you've been with before him. That means that you have not divorced or let go of their size. As long as you hold on to those memories, your husband may not measure up or stand a fighting chance for the real first place in your heart. And the real deal is that their size doesn't and cannot matter when you are with your God-given husband. Let it go.

Don't get caught up with wanting to be familiar with the anatomy of another man – his body, his bank, his life and what he has to offer you – that you miss the divine connection between you and the one God wants you to be with. This is not about who you want to be with. This is completely about who God has for you. The wedding vows say, "What God has put together, let no man put asunder." That includes the man in your head, sister. You can't afford to get caught up with the fantasy of another man when you have the real one standing in front of you. It is an insult to God to push away the one He has prepared for you when he doesn't measure up to the one in your head.

How dare you push away a man who is working day and night to prove to you that he's a man of integrity to be with a fine dude who doesn't work? Just because he's fine and everybody wants him does not make him worthy of you. It does not get him out of his mother's basement. He may be fine and drive a fancy car but he still lives in the hood. He doesn't have a bank account. He has to get his checks cashed at the liquor store. But you'd rather have that than the man who's working three jobs and has a bank account. You'd rather have that than to drive around in his smaller car right now. You'd rather choose the dude in the Benz or the Jeep even though he lives with his mama.

How dare you believe God for a husband and be offended when he finds you and gives you something small that he can afford? Because you and your girls are used to watching reality television, with unrealistically big rocks on their hands. You emasculate this good man who is doing his best in this moment. What makes it okay for you to make him think he's not good enough? So what he had to go to KMart or Walmart to get the best ring he could get? He loves you so much that he chose to be with you and nobody else. And because he loves you, he's didn't want to take out a $5,000 loan to get you a rock. He'd rather put that money aside to save as a down payment on your first house together. So he spent $200 on the ring he gave you instead of going into unnecessary debt. When we have these attitudes, we're teaching our men that size does matter. We're teaching them how judgmental and shallow we can be.

We've got to get our priorities straight, ladies. Do you want the big ring now or do you want the husband with the savings account? He's gonna put some money away for your kids. He's gonna have an insurance policy. He pays his tithes and offering. He knows how to respect and love you and his family. He's not gonna leave you home sick with the kids; he's gonna stay home with you. He's not gonna spend more time with the boys than he does with his family. He understands he's a husband first.

You want a man of God that will cover you, protect you, listen to you, submit to you, and band around you. What does that mean? Look at your ring. Its shape is a circle. Your husBAND is the band around your family which is placed in the center of the circle. He bands like a covering around them for safety and protection. He protects you from intruders and intrusion. He protects in the spirit and in the natural. The husband that is given to you by God takes that position very seriously. He assures that no hurt or harm comes to you. He places his very existence on the line for his family. And when praying and believing God he is covering his family. Size doesn't matter when you are talking about the husband God has prepared for you.

Now let's really talk about size.

Some of you think that if he's not well endowed, he has a problem. I'm here to tell you, he doesn't. Do you think God was taken by surprise with how He blessed your man? Do you think your man stood in line and asked for an extra small thingy? He didn't pick that. And after all, what is "well endowed" anyway? How many inches does that measure up to be exactly?

The problem is that most of you are coming in to this thing with information you are not supposed to have. You've got some preconceived ideas about what it's supposed to be to be acceptable. And you're holding him accountable for your misinformation. You learned some things fornicating, watching porn, and using dildos and toys. None of which you were supposed to be doing. And now you have the nerve to tell him, he's not big enough to satisfy you.

Let's bottom-line some things here. You think that it is size that's gonna get you "there." Not so much. (Brace yourself for a reality check here.) Women need direct clitoral stimulation. You need your husband to put his mouth on you and his fingers on you to get you there. Size has nothing to do with any of that. The marriage bed is undefiled. What happens between you and your husband is blessed by God. He created sex and desires us to be familiar in the most intimate of ways. We become one flesh. I am his and he is mine. I know my husband's body as well as I know my own and he knows mine. God created sex for husbands and wives, not for "Boohs" and "Baes."

So ladies, if you made your man feel like he wasn't good enough, you owe him an apology. If you made him feel in any way like he wasn't enough – his money wasn't enough, his education wasn't enough, his car wasn't enough – and he's doing his absolute best, you ought to apologize to him. Lift him up instead of tearing him down. Tell him how much you appreciate him instead of how much you wish he were different.

Start calling him a Man of God. Just start affirming it. As it is in the spirit realm so it is in the natural. Start calling him, "Man of God." Tell him how much you appreciate who he is to you and how he treats you. Tell him how much you appreciate his leadership and his being the Head of the Household. Watch how God transforms his heart right before your eyes. Begin to pray for him and with him that he is the man God created him to be.

What really happens here is that your eyes and heart are transformed in the process. You stop focusing on everything he's not and begin to see everything he is and always has been. What you focus on, you get more of. How about that? What you focus on, you get more of. The Word of God says, if you keep your mind stayed on Jesus, He'll keep you in perfect peace (Isaiah 26:3). Focus on the peace of the Lord and you have more peace. When your mind is stayed on Jesus, you can't be complaining about what you think your man is lacking, can you? Size doesn't matter. Appreciation and focus do.

Now about this man that I so adore and love.

When he proposed to me it was Christmas Eve. We had been together for a couple of years. I had just had Josiah, which means I was out of wedlock and out of the will of God. I was hurting and rebellious. But Shaun and I worked things out. I didn't think that we were gonna get married because of some of the chaos we had been through. But Shaun surprised me. It was a little after 11:00pm Christmas Eve and he read me a poem. I sat on his lap and after he finished the poem, he presented me with a ring.

Now this is not my first marriage, but it is my perfect marriage. My first marriage was in God's permissive will, not His perfect will. In the first wedding I had the big dress, the six-foot train, the frilly dress, the $20,000 reception, limos and Corvettes and the big rock. And I paid for that ring dearly with a fool that cheated on me and abused me and left me for days at a time in a city where I knew no one. I really had no business marrying that man.

But now, God had reconnected me with my best friend, Shaun. He made up his mind that he was not going to be part of a generational curse anymore. And he gave me a band ring. No diamonds, no gems at all. Just silver with gold cuts. And I thought it was the most beautiful ring in the world. And I cried and I cried and I cried. I jumped up and down. I couldn't wait to marry him. Now, eight years later, I have gone from a band with gold cuts in it to a bridal set to what I wear now, two-and-a-half carats worth of diamonds. I want you to know that God wants big things for you. It might come in stages. It might come after a while. It might come, maybe later.

Don't make that man think he has to take out a second mortgage on your home so you can walk around with a rock right away. Love him where he is and he'll work his butt off to get you this. You want it right. You want it to be blessed. You want to have your priorities straight. You want to be able to grow together and accomplish some stuff together.

Father, in the name of Jesus, I just thank you for what
you are doing for these sisters. We give you the glory
for freedom. We thank you in advance for deliverance.
No hindrance. No straps. Nothing binding us to our
past. Thank you for the indwelling of the Holy Ghost.
We are glad to walk in the fullness of our freedom.
In the mighty name of Jesus.

Amen

This will be a time of breakthrough. Begin to decree
and declare breakthrough even before you see or experience it.
It begins with the expectation of it. Know this: if He can do it
for me, He can most certainly do the same or better for you. I
feel Him as I write this and prepare for this time together.
We're going to uncover the real marriages some of you are
engaged in and have been for a long time. You may have never
thought about it in this way before, but this will bless you.

So the question is: who are you married to? And I know
some of you are saying, "Markita, I'm married to my
husband." And some others of you are saying, "I'm not married
at all yet." Well, I'm here to tell you that some of you are
illegally married in the spirit. That means that you have
ungodly soul connections, or soul ties to people that you are
not married to. You have spiritual connections to people from

your past that are ungodly. Some of you are so stuck in your past that you can't even embrace your now. Some of you want to be married and want to be a good wife. The reason you haven't been able to do that is because you are so used to doing it in the ungodly way you have been outside of the will of God. And that way hasn't worked. Many of you are still married to your past.

And so God gave me a great revelation on how some of his daughters are still very much so married. He said you are married in the spirit and married through connections, sexual and non-sexual. Some connections are just mental. Some are just emotional. Others were just verbal contracts. We have made vows to people that we should never have made vows to. We made promises that God never intended for us to make to people we should not have been making promises to.

The problem is that you've never denounced those promises and never broken them. You've begun to start living from them. They still exist in your soul. You never asked God to forgive you for it. You never asked God to deliver you from it. You never said, "God I was out of your will. I was not doing things within your perfect will. I was in the permissive realm or being very emotional. I was being very naive to the devices in the enemy and therefore made a covenant with someone I should never have been in covenant with." We all have made connections to people that we should never have had any connection to. Every last one of us has said, "I got you. If no one else got you…I got you." We all have done it. It comes completely from our flesh and God's permissive will. We have all promised, "I'm never going to leave you, babe. No matter what. No matter what, you'll always be mine." We've all said something similar to this. No matter where or when you move, this person will always have a piece of your heart. We prophesied that foolishness. We get caught up saying, "No matter who you're with, you'll always be my man. No matter where you go, you'll always be my girl." And then we wonder why we can never get over an individual. Or we see a picture and flash back. Or we have a memory and we stay and think about yesteryear. We reminisce too long.

And we feel those same feelings all over again. I need you to know that you are still married to every one of those people. And I want to let you know that God wants us to be completely free. He wants us to be completely free, not somewhat free, not a little bit free, but completely free.

He needs you to see that, number one, it is a trick of the enemy. And number two, you think you have the strength and courage to move on from it on your own and you don't. And number three, that it is a device to try to keep you bound. It makes you say, "I'm over it," and you're really not.

So I want you to just think about the men and the relationships that you have been in. And think about how many times you said, "No matter what, I'll always be here. No matter what, you will always have a piece of my heart. No matter what, I'm always going to be your girl or you're always going to be my guy." Just think about it. It's time to get really honest with ourselves.

I did that. How many times, I did that. Because I'm loyal. And it meant something to me to be that kind of loyal. So if I'm with you I'm with you. And you will probably have to break up with me before I break up with you because I'm just that type of woman. If I was with somebody I was with somebody.

Then I went through the rejection and the rebellion. I was just totally outside of God's will. I was bouncing around from man to man. And then I got in real trouble because I was always angry. I was depressed. I wasn't suicidal but I easily could have been because I had all of this stuff in me. All of these men's spirits were in me, connected to me. Their fluids were in me. I would wake up one day just angry because I slept with someone that had anger issues. I would wake up sometimes really, really feeling icky because the body I dealt with was just nasty. I would wake up sometimes just really, really sad because somebody I was dealing with was always on an emotional rollercoaster. I laid down with these demons…willingly. Intentionally. I did that.

It wasn't until I had a one-on-one with the Lord and I said, "God what is this?" He said, "You made a covenant with people. When you became one with them you made covenant with them." And that is Truth. When we lay down sexually with people we become one with them whether it's the will of God or not for our lives. We come into agreement with them. And so now you have opened yourself up to receive whatever is in that person. You agree with their stuff at a cellular level. You embraced and accepted their stuff as your own. Some of you have made verbal connections and verbal vows to people with whom you had no business doing that.

In my course, the Wifely Way, we teach you that God is preparing us for marriage. We want our husbands to find us being who we are in God. Except they can't find us because we have made a connection and come into agreement with another man. And no matter how much you want to protest and disagree that you are married to the other man it doesn't change the fact that according to heaven you are. In the spirit you are. You've got to take ownership of that. It is the only way to be delivered and healed from your past.

Some of us have been molested. Some of us have been raped. Some of us have been abused. We've been in and out of relationships trying to fit in. We want them to love us and want them to be there. And then when they don't work out we blame them because we say in our mind we did everything right. In actuality we did not. We did not do everything right.

And then we deal with some of the consequences. And I'm not saying we're playing victim. What I am saying is that we've got to be accountable for the things that we did agree to. We are accountable for some of the hurt, the pain, the frustrations, the shame and the humiliation that came when we chose to be intertwined with these people. We made that decision out of our flesh, apart from the will of God. And that's what we should never have done.

So now we have to ask God to help us and to realign us and prepare us for a divorce. I know, you're saying, God doesn't like divorce. No He does not like divorce but that doesn't change the fact that these marriages that He also doesn't like have to end.

So we ask God now to prepare us for the separation. Help us with the annulment.

I'm going to bring you to the Word of God about knitting souls together and soul ties and things of that nature. First Samuel 18:1: "As soon as he had finished speaking to Saul, the soul of Jonathan was knit to the soul of David, and Jonathan loved him as his own soul." That is an example of knitting a soul together or the intertwining of souls together. David and Jonathan became covenant brothers. They weren't blood brothers but they became covenant brothers and so they made a vow to each other. That is an example of a soul connection. They made a covenant vow to each other. All soul ties or connections are not perverse. They're not sexual. That is important to know. You can have a soul connection without having a sexual relationship. It's about the emotional, mental connection between people.

Here's another example of a soul tie. Let's look at Hebrews 4:12: "For the Word of God is living and active, sharper than any two-edged sword piercing to the division of the soul and of the spirit of joint and of marrow and discerning thoughts and intentions of the heart." This is all spirit connection. Now here is an example of the immoral soul tie. 1 Corinthians 6:18: "Flee from sexual immortality. Every other sin a person commits outside the body, but the sexual immoral person sins against his own body." This is especially for the wives. Genesis 2:24: "Therefore a man shall leave his father and mother and hold fast or cleave to his own wife and they shall become one flesh." Pay attention to this: Genesis 2:24: "And therefore a man shall leave his father and his mother and hold fast or cleave to his own wife and they shall become one flesh." Here again is the husband and wife coming together.

The highest form of worship between a husband and a wife is not them lifting their hands in worship. You know, speaking in tongues and praising and dancing and falling out.

The highest form of worship for husband and wife, the highest works of the husband and wife, is when they come together in sexual intercourse. That's why it is important that you do not open yourself up to being with just any body. I really need you to hear me on this. I want you to hear my heart when I say it is not okay to test the waters. It's not OK to do things the way the world does. It's not OK for you to try to see if he's big enough; if he can take you there. It's not OK for you to give your body to somebody that it doesn't belong to because then when you marry, you start thinking about your exes. Trust me on this. I'm not telling you something I heard about or that someone told me. I'm telling you the truth I've lived through. When I got married, I had to fight the images of my exes. I had to fight the thoughts of where I used to be with other men while I was married.

I had to ask God, "I love my husband. I'm in love with my husband. My husband gets me there. My husband rock's my boat. He makes me feel all kinds of good inside. Why has that image come back? I don't want that." God said that spirit is still in you. That really kind of blew me away! I couldn't imagine that person was still with me. I asked God, "What do you mean that spirit is still in me?" He said, "You did not call their name out. You did not cut the ties. You did not denounce it. You did not break it. You did not sever it. You did not come against it. That means that person is still in you." You may not

79

even remember their name. But because you didn't ask God to deliver you, they're still inside of you. Some people don't believe in that. There are some people that are just dumb enough to believe that spiritual deposits are not real.

Spirits transfer. That is truth.

And some of you are walking around angry at your husband, blaming him for what somebody did to you two or three years ago, ten years ago, twenty years ago. And you don't understand why it makes you mad when your husband does a certain thing. It makes you mad because homeboy did that and you forgot about it.

You forgot about it but your spirit didn't forget about it. Your flesh forgot about it, your intellect forgot about it, your conscious forgot about it but your subconscious didn't forget it. It's still back there thinking, "Why don't I like it when you wear that? I picked it out." What you don't remember is that you picked it out for somebody else and when you got mad at that person you didn't like that outfit anymore.

This is why it is important before you get married to be honest with yourself. To be honest with God and say, "God anything in me, even the things I don't remember. If it's not of you, if there's not a Godly connection, if it's not ordained, not healthy, then get it out of me."

I had a one-on-one with the Lord. I had a conversation with God and I began to write down names and call out to God.

And I began to cry. I slept with this person. I touched this person. I stayed on the phone too long with this person. I had a mental connection with this person and I gave too much information about me to this person. I let this person in too much. I made a covenant vow with this person. God get them out of me please. And I began to cry.

I began to actually count the names. And then there were some people I forgot about. I told God whatever it takes, whatever it is, I don't want to bring this into my Now. I don't want to bring this into my now situation. I don't want to bring this to my current situation. This is not fair to my husband.

The Bible says while we're on this earth our days are full of trouble; I don't want to add to that. I want to enjoy my husband. And for you single ladies: you want to enjoy your life while you're single. You can still date. You can still enjoy yourself. You could still go out and have a good old time. But when you start adding sex and impure thoughts and when you're having perverted conversation you are entering dangerous territory. And some of you are saying, "I don't fornicate. I don't have sex." But you are having impure thoughts, impure conversation. Some of you are even engaging in self-gratification, touching yourself and pleasing yourself. And that's out of God's will. It's perversion. What are you thinking about? You have to be honest with yourself to be free from it. It's a trap to keep you from your full potential to be a good wife.

A good wife is not a woman that sits in the corner and is just hush. A good wife is not a woman who just sits around waiting for her husband to tell her what to do. She does not kowtow to her husband. Even though I have no problem doing whatever he likes, that's not all there is to me and that is not all there is to you.

"Yes. Whatever you want. Whatever you want, dear." No! You are not a sex slave either. You want to bring all that you are to your husband. Everything that God had placed in you before he came is what you want to bring into the marriage. You don't lose your voice just because you got married. You are still you and bringing all of who you are enhances the joining together of the two of you. And to you single women, you want to be sure of who you are and certain that you know who you are. In a previous chapter we dealt with who you are. And we dealt with knowing who God said you are. If you knew who you were, if you really knew who you were, you wouldn't just let everybody fool with you. Talk to you any kind of way. You wouldn't compromise so much. You wouldn't fall for the trick. You would have so much self-respect and value that no one could take that place with you except your husband.

If you really knew who you were you wouldn't put limitations on yourself. So we learned that we don't have to be the side-chick. We learned that we are not a "wifey" but a wife. Do you know who you are? Do you know that God calls you Favored? Do you know that you are a treasure? And until he finds you, you should remain hidden. Hidden doesn't mean that you are buried so deep that no one can find you, but it certainly means that not everybody should have access to you. You've got to know your value. Everybody can't touch you.

Everybody can't converse with you. And that is not you being stuck-up. You are guarding yourself because you don't want to come into contact with things that are not of God. You do not want to come into covenant with things and people and spirits that are not healthy, that are not of God. That would be to your detriment. Hear me well on this. It would be to your detriment. I never understood why I would see young ladies having babies with guys who had 30 babies already. And she is really thinking that if she has his baby he won't treat her the same way. I do not understand what she is thinking!

Then the Lord showed me that every woman he slept with she slept with too. Every woman he deposited into, he grabbed to their spirit and she grabbed to his. So when he lay down with another woman, the same thing happened over again. He grabbed her spirit and she grabbed his. And it was a ripple effect that just kept going with each new person. So all the women thought the same thing. All the women said the same thing: "He won't do that to me. I'm different. He really loves me. He even said so. I can take care of his kids. I'm not like those others he left. I can change him. He just needs somebody to understand him." Now we're talking ten, fifteen kids later, he's still sleeping around. He's got a new woman saying, "He won't do that to me." You've adopted that spirit. You've taken that so-called "truth" and made your own story. And now it has manifested in you. I ask women all the time, "Why would you stay with someone that's hitting you?" They all say, "Because he loves me." I ask, "Why do you believe that?" "Because my mom used to get hit and my dad loved her." So that's the explanation? These are things that you really believe and have come into agreement with and made true for you. You have come into agreement with things that are not holy. Then you wonder why you go through what you go through.

You've got to be able to hear this truth. You have got to be able to accept the truth for what it is and apply it to your life. You cannot be afraid to face the real facts and take responsibility for it, be accountable for it. You have the chance to get it right today, right now. It is not God's will for your life to just be pulled under and suffocated. It's not His will for you. You have the chance right now to start over, start fresh. You've got to forgive. You've got to denounce these people. You've got to let the ungodly relationships go in order for you to be the greatest wife you could ever be. Because being a great wife has nothing to do with just being pretty and having sex and being silent. Being a bad wife is not just about opening up your mouth and being disrespectful and rolling your neck and not cooking and cleaning. Some of you are bad wives because you don't tell your husband the truth. Some of you are bad wives because you don't hold your husband accountable to the vision. Some of you are bad wives because you won't pray for your husband.

The term "soul tie" is not used in the Bible. It discusses souls being knit together, becoming one flesh. Essentially, the soul tie exists in the spirit realm and brings two people together. For married couples, it is an almost magnetic pull between them that draws them together.

Soul ties that develop between fornicators can draw a beaten and abused woman to an abusing partner. He treats her like trash and doesn't love her. Even so, she turns to him for validation and regard that she will never receive. It's demonic.

How are soul ties formed?

These are some of the ways I know of that soul ties are formed:

The number one way is through sexual relations. Godly soul ties are formed between a married couple according to Ephesians 5:31, "For this cause shall a man leave his father and mother and shall be joined or cleave to his wife. And the two shall become one flesh." And a godly soul tie between a husband and wife as God intended is for it to be unbreakable. However when a person has ungodly relationships with other people, an ungodly soul tie is formed. "What know ye not which ye have joined to a harlot? Now as one body." Do you know what a harlot is? Harlot is whore, slut, or nasty girl. Freak. Trick. This soul tie fragments the soul and is destructive. People who have many past relationships find it very difficult to bond or be joined to anybody because their soul is fragmented.

Close relationships is another way soul ties are formed. For example, King David and Jonathan had a good soul tie as a result of good friendship. "So it came to pass that when he made an end of speaking unto Saul that the soul of Jonathan was knit unto the soul of David. And Jonathan loved him as his own soul."

Bad soul ties can come from bad relationships as well. Idolizing someone can form a bad soul tie. Conversation can cause a bad soul tie. Imagine that you know somebody is trifling, or out of order. You know someone is ignorant. You know someone is foolish. You know someone is mean, manipulative, demonic, and you still commit to them, telling them, "No matter what, I got you." You just made a soul tie to that person.

How do you break a soul tie?

You break a soul tie by denouncing that person. You break a soul tie by asking God to sever, break and deliver. Every time you ask God to get them out of you, He does it. He moves. It happens quickly. He does it because He knows you're serious about being in right relationship with Him and about breaking the soul ties you created through your flesh. This is why God wants us to present our bodies as a living sacrifice, holy unto Him and acceptable. This is why they that worship Him must worship Him in spirit and in truth. Not in some truth, not in part of a truth, not in lies. Not in tipping around, always repenting. You repent every day about the same thing. You're not delivered. You need to be delivered. My mother used to say, "I smell sin on you," and just look at me and walk away. No matter how many times I would take a shower. No matter how many times I soaked. No matter how many times I bleached my skin. Or tried to scrub that stuff off, she would still sniff around me, smellin' sin on me. How did she know? That's how God looks at us. Every time we fall. Stop falling! Don't open up the door to sin, fall into sin, get up, dust yourself off and start walking again, only to fall in again. Stop falling in the first place so you can be the best wife you can be!

Now pay attention…not everyone will be married. And shame on wives who look down on women who are not married. Truth be told, some of us should not have gotten married when we did. So stop that too! I minister to single women who do not want marriage yet still want to enjoy their lives. You can do that and still not practice sexual sin. There are still some women out there that are pure and not fornicating. Know that.

So here is how to break soul ties:

1. Worship – that is the strongest thing you could ever do. You must get into the spirit to worship.

2. Repentance – "God forgive me." You've got to ask with sincerity and seriousness. Not with the intention to do the same thing all over again.

3. Denounce the person – Ask God to cleanse you of that person's spirit, flesh, and essence.

It's funny. I don't remember who they are. I don't remember what they looked like. I don't remember where I was. But I remember the scent. I remember the moment. I remember the feeling that I felt. I remember ten years ago, nine years ago, a couple of months ago, last week, I remember that. And I don't like how that makes me feel on the inside. "Whatever that is, God you know what it is. Get it out of me. Create in me a clean heart and renew a right spirit within me. Cast me not away from your presence." A sinner cannot be in the presence of God. A sinner can be in the presence of Jesus, but not in the presence of God. Even in the Old Testament when the priests had to go behind the veil, they had to wear bells at the bottom of their garment. If there was any sin on them at all, they would drop dead in the presence of God. We're talking about the priests that were in the synagogue, in the temple. Any sin on them, they would immediately drop dead. They would be dragged out from behind the veil by a rope wrapped around their waist.

When the burning bush was going, God said to Moses, "Take off your sandals. This is holy ground. You can't bring that stuff before Me. I am God."

So we have to repent of doing ungodly things. You have to ask God to forgive you for making these connections to people. Forgive you for decisions you made because you felt badly in your heart for them. Nobody else wanted to be their friend. And you wanted to be their friend. They didn't have anybody else. And now we have to ask God to break it.

And I'm not talking about breaking chains here. Soul ties are not chains. A chain can come back together. You know that if you've ever had a necklace and it came apart. You got some pliers and pulled the link apart to hook it back together. We're not talking about chains here. We're talking about spirit breaking off my life. God, snatch it out of me. I don't want that anymore because I want to be a great wife. I want to submit to my husband.

It was hard for me to submit to my husband because the last man that I was with made me feel less than, like I was a slave. Or like I was beneath him. The last person that I was with made me feel insignificant. They made me feel like I wasn't an achiever. It crushed me. Now that I'm married to this person, I always fight. I'm always trying to prove who I am. Because I really want to fight the person that made me feel this way. But I didn't have enough strength to fight that person. So before I let you come up on me I'm gonna fight you first. I'm gonna swing first. I already know what you're gonna say, so before I let you get one more word out, I'm gonna attack. Even though that person has not come to fight. It's time to let go of what came before and the expectation of a fight.

Be honest. You talk to your husband crazy! You put your husband through hell. And he's not going to tell you because every time he tries to tell you, he hears you on the phone dragging him through some more. So since he can't tell you, I will. Hush! Watch how you talk to him. Some of you are just downright mean! You would never talk to the person who made you feel that way in the first place this way. So why are you doing it to the one that loves you the most? We're talking about doing things the Wifely Way.

We want to get completely free from our past. So we can embrace and enjoy where we are. And enjoy being married. I'm going to challenge some of you wives to go to your husbands tonight and apologize. And apologize sweetly. "Baby, I'm sorry. I've been talking to you all kinds of crazy." Now he's probably going to think that you are trying to kill him. So don't ask him about the insurance policy tonight. He's probably going to look at you like, "What did you put in the food?" Just assure him that you're not trying to kill him. Be sincere and tell him again that you apologize for talking to him crazy. Then tell him that you know you weren't over some things. You don't have to go into detail. He already knows you're nuts and he loves you anyway. Just tell him that there are some areas where you thought you were healed and you really weren't. And you took it out on him and you're really sorry. And give him a hug and kiss. Some of you can do a little bit more. And build from there. Appreciate that man and let him know you gonna get this thing right. And be excited about it. Then start doing things the Wifely Way. Stop withholding from your husband. Stop putting him on punishment. That is foolish and stupid.

If you are single, there is no reason you don't have a passport. You need to be travelling outside of your city, region and state. If you are single, you need to start doing things outside of your neighborhood. You are so good at saying there are no good men out there. Of course there are. They are just outside of your area. You may have to go where they are. Even when you are dating online, you can develop a soul tie with somebody. You may not be fornicating but you are on there, flirting, sending pictures and talking nasty. You are still intertwining with these people. That's developing a soul tie. You have to break the soul ties so that God can send you the right man.

I would be willing to bet you have at some time in your life created a list of qualities that you want in your husband. Am I right? Be honest. And most of the stuff on your list was shallow and petty. You wanted someone tall, dark and handsome. He had to have swag like Denzel or Idris. He had to be suave like Blair Underwood. He had to have just the right smile and the right build like Dwayne "The Rock" Johnson. He had to make you laugh like Kevin Hart. He had to smell right and sound right with a deep, sexy voice that would whisper the right words in your ear.

Okay, dream time is over. He's probably not gonna have any of that. I can pretty much guarantee it. You left off the most important aspects of your husband. You need to start the list with how much he loves God and loves you the way God created him to love you. Add that he prays with and for you daily. Add that he is considerate and kind and thoughtful. Add that his character is strong and solid. Add that he respects and admires you. Add that he is highly regarded in the community and at his workplace. Add that he has a generous heart. Now you've started a list that has meat and promise. All that other is nice, but it is not lasting. It is not the stuff upon which a strong marriage is built.

———⟨○⟩———

Throughout this whole journey we've been talking about how women every day completely destroy themselves trying to get married at best, or trying to just have a man, any man, at worst. We have all seen women demean themselves and the God in them by wearing revealing clothes, going to clubs and bars trying to be chosen. The pain and desperation of their brokenness and loneliness compel them into worldly ways of finding a partner hoping for a spouse. This only leads to more heartache and despair. Then comes Sunday morning, they stand ashamed before God. The Holy Spirit convicts them in God's presence. We talked about how sin cannot dwell in the presence of God's perfect holiness. We praise Him for the gift of repentance, though we should not be repenting for the same thing over and over and over and over again.

I know it's hard. I've been there. And what I know is that there can be joy in the waiting. Let's be honest…do you really want the one you found in the bar, you know the one that just bought you drinks and maybe danced with you? Meanwhile he's buying drinks for her, her and maybe him too! What makes you think he'll marry, honor and respect you when you looked like a harlot when he met you? You remember what a harlot is, right? And now that you got his attention, you want to dress conservatively and go to church with him. Not.

Are Christians supposed to find their spouse in the bar? Are they supposed to find them in the church? I will say this: just because he goes to church or serves in church doesn't mean he's your husband. Stop thinking you're going to change him into the Godly King your heart wants him to be. And be real, if you are following God and devoted to serving Him with your life, then marrying a non-believer is not even close to being an option. By the way, I am not only referring to the unsaved woman. Some saved women just wear me out. Hiding behind church all the while just as confused and grasping at straws too. I have seen religious women settle and I wanted to just grab them and say, "Get out of this! This isn't God's best." I knew a woman very close to me and she was married for many years to a man who she felt "loved" her. He played so many emotional games with her. I witnessed him go through her money, verbally abuse her, threaten to leave her at any given moment and she suffered through that anyway. For years he wouldn't even be intimate with her and I would ask her, "Why are you with someone who doesn't love you?" She always replied, "I love him and trust God." Well that man never changed. They are not together anymore and I know she's in a better place. She's actually resting in the arms of the Lord. That's right; it took death for her to have peace. Don't let that be you. Don't trick yourself into thinking "staying" with someone who isn't willing to change means you're in the will of the Lord either.

A popular marriage scripture is Proverbs 18:22: "Whoso findeth a wife findeth a good thing and obtaineth favor from the Lord." Based on this scripture, women have repeatedly been admonished to "be the good thing he finds." Be the wife. That's what we've been talking about in this work.

It is proven science that men benefit from marriage. The Proverbs 18:22 passage refers to the institution of marriage being the good thing he finds. It didn't say, "When he finds a woman." It didn't say, "When he finds a partner." It didn't say, "When he finds a girlfriend, a lover, a mistress." It specifically states that he who finds a "wife" finds a good thing and obtains favor from the Lord. As his wife, you are part of the favor he finds.

We've covered a lot of ground in this work so far. And now we need to apply what we've learned. After all, we're in this to make life look and be different, more like what brings us joy in the Lord and in the home. What is the point if nothing in your life changes or you still don't feel like you have what you need to have the manifest blessings of the Lord?

We talked a little bit about the extraordinary qualities of the Virtuous Woman and the responsibilities of a wife. A huge part of that responsibility is to be someone he wants to find. We talked about being the hidden treasure. Hidden treasure is worth finding. Work on becoming the woman a godly Christian man would want to find…and marry. Of course that starts with the desire to be a godly wife.

This is serious. The Word of God says, "Seek ye first the kingdom of God and His righteousness, and all these things shall be added unto you" (Matthew 6:33). The added unto you includes the godly husband. But look at what it says first. It's not enough to want to be a godly wife to have the husband. The desire to please and know God intimately has to come first and it has to stand alone. Remember we said that in your marriage God comes first for both of you? That starts here. You have to first desire a relationship with God, seeking Him, loving Him, wanting more of Him, and desiring to please Him before the godly husband will come. This is also related to knowing who you are.

Ask God in this process to show you to you as He sees and knows you. It will blow your mind! When sometimes all we can see is all that's wrong, He sees us through His perfection in us. He says that when we repent and ask forgiveness of our sins, He throws them as far away from us as the east is from the west (Psalm 103:12). He throws them into the depths of the sea (Micah 7:19) where they exist no more. We focus on our mistakes. He sees only His forgiveness. We focus on everything we got wrong. He sees only how much He loves us. Be still and know that He is God and His mercy is enough to cover all of your wrongs. I challenge you to spend some of your private time with Him asking Him to show you how He regards you. Then embrace that Truth as your own.

So here's the plan…become the godly wife that is the found treasure. Create the person of "wife" now and the godly man will be presented to you. I'm not talking about "acting as if" or faking it 'til you make it here. I mean become the wife that you want to be with the qualities and characteristics she would have. Not faking it, being it.

Would a godly wife go clubbing on the regular? Would a godly wife eat out every day? Would a godly wife publically wear revealing clothes? Would a godly wife lie, cheat and argue? Would a godly wife be suspicious of her husband? Would a godly wife cause strife in her household? Would a godly wife skip prayer and time with the Lord to be on the phone gossiping? Would a godly wife allow her home to be cluttered and disorganized? Would a godly wife allow the laundry to pile up? Would a godly wife talk about her husband's faults with her friends? Would a godly wife disrespect her marriage vows? Would a godly wife expect her husband to be a mind-reader? Would a godly wife displace her emotions and blame her husband for her disappointments? Would a godly wife set different standards for her husband than she maintains for herself?

Are you beginning to get the picture?

A godly wife has a certain character. Not only is she capable of maintaining a home and several businesses, but she has a certain personality as well. She is kind and considerate of her husband and everyone else. Now this is not to say that she is a pushover. She is not that by any means. She picks her fights, so to speak. She doesn't have to go ghetto to get her point across. She is eloquent of speech, though able to break it down when she needs to.

She is reliable and disciplined. She is interesting and engaging. She is encouraging and builds up rather than pulls down. She is stable and steady. She has excellent communication skills and uses them proficiently. She isn't quick to judge. The godly wife is not prone to flying off the handle. She doesn't make assumptions. It never ceases to amaze me how many women make assumptions about everything.

If they don't have an answer, they make one up to suit what they already believe. And why is that always something negative? If you don't know, then ask. If they can't tell you, have enough patience to help them tell you. You already know that many men are not verbal in how they express themselves. They aren't used to talking, much less talking about their feelings. Be patient. Be loving. Be there for them without jumping to conclusions and forcing them to explain themselves. If you create a safe place for them to talk, they will. But if every time you say you want to talk, it means they're about to get a beat down, you're going to get a shut down. They may show up but it's going nowhere. Be a soft place to land. Not a land mine. If you don't know how to communicate well, find a community college class or a business seminar on developing interpersonal skills. It could go a long way in your relationship.

A godly wife is disciplined in living her life. I don't mean regimented. Being regimented is like being religious. You know those church services where everything has to happen at a certain time in a certain way. There is no leeway for a move of the Holy Ghost. He can't have his way in that kind of atmosphere. In fact, he's probably nowhere near that church. Being disciplined means being purposeful, being focused, being intentional. A godly wife is intentional and purposeful in her life. She's not a victim of circumstance and life isn't something that just happens to her.

A godly wife is accountable for her behavior and choices. She says what she means and doesn't talk just to be talking. She is consistent in who she is. Not one way with one group and another way with someone else. People who know her trust her and know that her intention is never self-serving but she always means the best for everyone. She is transparent in her purpose and never has ulterior or hidden motives.

The godly wife is settled. She is able to be still and quiet. She's grounded and a pleasure to be around. Her presence brings peace and life to the atmosphere. She is not attention-seeking, though ironically attracts attention with her very essence. Her joy and centeredness are like a magnet. She is not the kind of person that people walk on eggshells around, never knowing what response or reaction they'll get, always watchful of what mood she may be in.

There is nothing desperate about the godly wife. So you singles, leave the partner seeking binoculars at home. Remember you reap what you sow. If you are sowing "I'm desperate for a man" seeds, you'll reap a harvest of men who will take advantage of that desperation. That's wifey energy. That's energy that just screams, "Use me, please!"

A godly wife is secure. She has high self-esteem and values herself. Like I said when we started, you have to know who you are. A godly wife knows she's not perfect and neither is her husband. But she knows what her issues are and has handled them. They don't have to be completely gone, either. We are all works in progress. But God is enough to make up for any shortcomings we have when we surrender them to Him. When we know what areas we still struggle with, we also know when and how they pop up. If you need help working through your stuff, then talk to your pastor or seek out a Christian counselor. There is help out there but you have to take the first step. Again you have to want it.

A godly wife is a good friend. She has healthy friendships that uplift and encourage her, and she them. She is able to keep appropriate confidences. She doesn't gossip and talk about people. She has healthy boundaries. She has friends that support her and honor the relationship with her husband. She sees the best in them and they in her. They trust each other implicitly and completely.

A godly wife is able to balance work and home. She places a priority on her time so that it is well spent. When she's working, she's working and when she's home, she's home. She is the authority on her family. She is attentive to the needs of each member and relates accordingly. If you are a mother, you know that each of your children is different and has different needs. One may be artistic, sensitive and contemplative while another may be precise, mathematical and decisive. Each requires a different language and way of parenting. They have different ways of hearing and relating to the world. A godly wife is aware of and celebrates this uniqueness.

A godly wife is mature, emotionally and spiritually. The Word says, "To whom much is given, much is required" (Luke 12:48). As a godly wife, there may be things that she has to overlook for the sake of peace. There may be things that she has to choose to respond to rather than react to. According to the Word of God, she returns no one evil for evil (Romans 12:17). She's not vindictive. She is forgiving. She lives life from a space of centeredness, not being triggered up all the time. When you're triggered up you are looking for a fight all the time. You're expecting it. And like a self-fulfilling prophecy, that is what happens. A godly wife knows, by discernment, that when someone is angry, it may not be what it appears to be. They may be speaking from their own pain and disappointment. When someone lashes out at her, she may not be the real problem at all and is smart and grounded enough to know that. And to go a step further, she is able to help the other person see the truth about their anger. How awesome is that?! It is truly a gift to be a godly wife.

This is part of the wisdom that a godly wife walks in. A definition of wisdom is having experience, knowledge and sound judgement. God's Word says for whoever lacks wisdom, to ask, and He will pour it out liberally (James 1:5). A godly wife seeks the Lord's wisdom in her decisions, her relationships, her attitudes and her opinions. Her desire is to be a sound representation of Christ in her life, and that means that she thinks through the mind of Christ. She is not driven by her emotions. She chooses what she spends her time thinking about and casts down imaginations and everything that raises itself up as a standard against the knowledge of God. This means that she controls and guides her thoughts and emotions. She chooses joy. She doesn't just think up stupid stuff and act on it. She's not reactionary. She knows that just because she thought it does not make it true. That's part of knowing herself and where she still has challenges and weaknesses.

A godly wife is kind. She is forgiving. She is thoughtful and considerate.

A godly wife knows God. She knows the sound of His voice and the move of His spirit. She is sensitive to the presence of God. She spends alone time with Him every day in her prayer closet and nurtures the relationship she has with Him. She regards Him in all that she does and holds her husband, family, business, church, decisions, and plans up before Him. She values His opinion and seeks His pleasure. She lives to hear Him say, "Well done, my good and faithful servant. Enter into the joy of the Lord" (Matthew 25:21).

Seeing this description of a godly wife may have just caused you to want to give up trying. You may be so overwhelmed by all of that that you want to just stop before you've even started! After all, who could possibly be all of that?! And if someone could, how long will it take to get there? It feels impossible.

The remarkable part of all of this is that God is able to create all of this in you. I am a living witness. With all that I've been through, being this kind of woman certainly did not come naturally for me. As I continued to walk with God and to surrender all of my hurt and pain to Him and to hold up this image of me before Him, over time He re-created me to be more and more of this kind of woman. It was not something that I could have done on my own. It never even occurred to me that this was available. But what I know of the God I serve is that because this is His desire for me, it became the desire of my heart and He gave me the desire of my heart.

Remember I said that Shaun and I really had a hard time when we got together. Neither one of us was who we are today. We had a lot to let go of and a lot of healing to do. And we did it together.

What you also need to know is that when you desire to be a godly wife, the man you desire changes too. If you really want to be this godly wife we've been talking about, then certainly God will bless it and present you with a man of God. Remember, God created marriage and it is good in His sight.

Should I stay in a physically abusive marriage?

> NO! Get out of there! If you are not getting help and he is not getting help and he is not changing, you need to leave that situation. Can God restore anything? Absolutely He can. Can God turn a man's heart from cheating? Absolutely. But it is not the will of God that you be verbally, physically, emotionally abused. God will take care of you. I know that.

Should we pray for desired intimacy with our future husband?

> Marriage is a gift. God honors marriage between husband and wife; sex is the gift! You want to have a great time with your spouse. The marriage bed is undefiled. People in the world have more sex than married couples and they feel free! We that are under "holy" matrimony should express pure passion and intimacy with our spouses. God created sex for marriage. He knows.

Do we need to denounce rape and molestation?

> Yes. Because when you have been violated and forced to do things against your will, there is a spirit of rejection and shame that will try to humiliate you and

make you feel like it was your fault. It wasn't your fault. So that is another trap of the enemy. It's deception and so you denounce that and come against it. How do I know? Because I was raped and molested. And I had to get that image out of my spirit. So I can talk about it freely because I am free. I'm able to identify with women who have gone through that because I've overcome it. I don't let that become a place of shame. I've overcome it and I'm victorious. Denounce that spirit. Don't feel dirty anymore. You're not dirty. That was not God's will. God didn't want that to happen to you. That was a sick person that was full of demons that did that to you and it was not your fault! Say that out loud: "It was not my fault!" Say it again...now say it again: "It was not my fault!" God was not in that. But He promised us that whatever the enemy meant for our bad He would turn it around for our good. So absolutely denounce rape and molestation. And I decree and declare: Father we thank you for freeing us from the shame of rape and the shame of molestation, being forced to do things at a young age or at any age. And we never told anybody or we told people and they didn't believe us, or they believed us but there were no consequences. God, I thank you right now for the freedom to move on from that and for the freedom to be healed as a testimony to be a blessing for someone else at the appointed time. In Jesus' name, amen. Be free from that. Don't let that cripple you another day. You will function. You will trust men, you will not think of that person on top you again. You will not think of that person who rubbed your breast and made you do things you should not have been doing. You will not be crippled by that. Not another day.

I have children with the person that I still struggle to not reminisce about every now and then. I know we weren't on the same page but sometimes I think back. I have to see him because of the children. How do I get past it?

You still have a soul tie with this person. When you have kids with someone you get connected with them. It does not mean that it has to be a soul tie. It does not have to be a spiritual connection. So you have to go through the steps I outlined earlier. Worship. Repent. Denounce that person: "God I respect this person. He is the father of my children. I care about this individual. But I don't want to be stuck in yesteryear with this person." And please, whatever you do, don't fall and sleep with him because he's your children's father. Remain pure before the Lord and He will bring you a husband that will love you and your kids. Don't fall for that kind of trap. "Teach me Lord, how to co-parent with him without lusting for him." Worship, repent, denounce. Say his name out loud. "Father, I thank you for taking the spirit of so-and-so out of my heart. I don't want every time he comes over for something to leap in me. Every time I see him something jumps in me." That's not God. That's your flesh. So don't get caught up and don't go the other way either. Don't hate him. You chose him.

If only I would have waited. I got married and could have been married to the man that God had for me. I listened to others when I got pregnant.

What you have to do is forgive yourself. And forgive the people that you are resenting right now. You have to forgive them because they thought they were doing what was best for you. But the Word says what the enemy meant for our harm God can turn around for our good. So I want you to think about all the great times you've had with these children and grandchildren. Ask God to help you recover and heal in those places that you still hurt.

What I know about God is that He already knows how we feel, so we can't be afraid to tell him how we feel. We have to not be afraid to tell him how we feel. To share this hurt with Him. I don't understand this. I don't like this. He said be angry and sin not. His ways are above our ways. He has ways that we don't know about we have to walk this thing out. Maybe life went this way to prevent you from going through something else. Just maybe. Embrace the journey that you went on. I want you to feel good about how you mothered these children and how you're an amazing grandmother. Do not allow the enemy to trick you into thinking you wasted time. Don't ever allow the enemy to make you think you have wasted time. Because God is a redeemer of time. The redeemer of time, He said we can recover. He'll replenish. He'll restore. Begin to think about those years and what you've endured and thank God that you were their mother. Thank Him that what you went through didn't kill you. I pray God will heal you in those places you hide so very well.

I have insecurities because I am divorced and have six children. It holds me back. Even though I have a lot to bring to the table, it holds me back.

God gave you those children because he trusted you. You didn't ask to go through a divorce. You didn't ask to be dropped and rejected. You didn't ask to have these children by yourself. It's not fair that you have six children now and you have to raise them. God never wanted that for you. But He does trust you to raise them. He is so awesome that He will still send you a man who can't have children. You need to hear me in the Holy Ghost. He can send you a man that wants children and who can't have them. What you have to start doing is bringing him forward: "God I thank you for the husband that you have sent me. I thank you that he's gonna love me and adore me and accept these as his children. God I thank you for preparing me and teaching me how to live with a man that didn't have children. Or who may have children and we are going to live harmoniously. We are going to break the stigma and blended families can get along. Thank you that my sons and daughters don't give me a hard time because mama has moved on. That they will have another father figure in their life." There are people out there who have a whole lot of kids and they still get remarried, and they embrace all the children as their own. We declare now that they will be your portion. God will send you a husband to care for you and for your children. And that they will receive him as a father and that it won't be hard. Bring no random men around your children until you know he's the one. Keep random men away from your babies. You will know he is the one. They should not see mama with random men. Don't limit God. He is able to send someone to you that will love you and your children. Unconditionally. I have an oldest daughter. I didn't give birth to her but she's mine, everywhere we go people say, "Your daughter looks just like you." I love this little girl so much that she has taken on aspects of me. I've known her since she was one year old. And I've cared for her as my first child. So I love her as if I had her out of my own belly. So there are men out there that will love you and your children. But you have got to love him and his children if he has children.

How do I help my Christian friends and family that are living in the wifey situation without coming across as judgmental?

Tell them this: "God never wanted that for you. He never wanted you to be somebody's wifey, "Booh" or "Bae." And you got to be able to tell them that you love them. At the end of the day people are going do what they want to. You can't force them. But you have a duty and obligation to tell them when they are in error. "I love you. You deserve better. It's not that he's a bad guy, you just keep thinking that one day he's gonna wake up and carry you away and he's not. You're not doing it God's way. You're doing it your way and you're praying that God will bless it." Okay, so I go into a store and I shoplift. And I take some clothes and stuff them in a bag and pray that nobody catches me. Please God don't let anybody see me. Please don't let anybody catch me. Please God bless me with these clothes. It's illegal and you're going to jail! And you want God to bless it. Please God bless this relationship. No, He's not. And if He does you are headed for rocky times, for sure. And marriage is already hard. It's already work and war and marriage. It comes with the package. So when you are disobedient, and out of order and out of God's way and his timing and all of that would add more trouble to it. So if you see a freight train headed at these people and you tell them to get off the tracks and they don't, then you have done your job. You have done what you were supposed to do and you keep it moving. You can't make people change their minds. You just present them with the truth. And that's not being judgmental. Being judgmental is this: "You going to hell if you don't stop. God ain't in that and you going to hell." There is a way to say it: "I'm really concerned. I'm really worried about you. I'm concerned. I don't think this is cool and I don't think this is right. I'm really going to be praying for you. This is not God's will. I love you." Always come back with compassion. "I love you. I'm just concerned." They will either receive you or not. Just love them.

I've always been told I'm ugly. It keeps me from being everywhere and with everyone. But no one knows. I thought I was in love.

Right now let me cancel out the lie, you are beautiful. I was told as a kid "you're ugly, you're fat, you're this, you're that. You're not light enough; your hair is not long enough; your teeth have gaps; you have a big butt," whatever. We have to cancel out the lies; the Bible says that we are fearfully and wonderfully made. I wish somebody would look me in my face and tell me I'm ugly. You must be smoking a new brand of crack. Look at yourself in the mirror and tell yourself, "I'm beautiful. There is something about every woman that is beautiful. It may be your eyes, cheekbones, bone structure, hips, breasts, legs, feet, hands, whatever, there is something beautiful about every last one of us. And you have to tap in to that place that no matter what anyone tells you, you know you are gorgeous. And another thing is that a little gloss never hurt anybody. A little bronzer on the cheek. A little mascara. I've seen some less attractive women have makeovers and there is something about a pallet and a brush.

Maybe you need to budget yourself and go to the department store makeup counter and have a makeover. I challenge some of you to do that. Go learn how to apply it to enhance your features. Take yourself to a Lancôme or a Mac counter and get some help. Stop watching YouTube if you don't know what you're doing. If they offer you samples accept. Don't buy anything if you can't afford it. Get your face done, take some pictures. Keep it in your phone, put it on social media, and say I just had a makeover. Put it up and look at it. See how beautiful you are. I don't want you thinking all the stars on TV are natural…that is weave; that is lashes; that is airbrush; that is botox; that is contouring; that is tattooed eyebrows; that is snatched noses; that is all fake. We're talking about butt pads, colored contacts, butt lifts, liposuction, implants, stage makeup, pounds of makeup. This is professional makeup applied professionally. What are you comparing yourself to? Who told you that you were ugly? Compared to who? I know girls that had to have their legs amputated trying to get butt implants. They allowed the media to tell them that the new body is a snatched waist and a round behind. If you weren't born with it, embrace what it is. Do some squats or not. And yes, the celebrities do have low self-esteem. I watched a video on people who are celebrities that have so much money they could wipe their behinds with it; they have so much and yet they are depressed and suicidal. They can buy anything, any house, any car, even friends and they're depressed. I believe they are depressed even from childhood. I still remember the things that people from my childhood said about me. Watch this. Those are the same people that need my help today. Those are the same people who look twice their age and I don't. Those are the same people who are addicted to drugs and alcohol, who are in bad, unhealthy relationships. They come to me so I can mother them. They come to me for prayer now. They come to me for the sister love that moves them back to where they need to be. I was never the pretty girl in the 6th, 7th, or 8th grade. And now, when I see the girls that were the pretty girls, I wonder what happened. The same people who do you wrong are the same people that will need you.

How do I let go of the feelings of loving a married man after I've said no and let go?

It's a soul tie. It was very brave of you to ask this question. Thank you for your trust. You know I will not judge you or give you false information. Let me say this: you are human. You have emotions and you have feelings. It was not right. It was absolutely positively wrong. However you are human and we are bound to make mistakes. However, we break from those things through the blood of Jesus. You cared for that person and you lay down with him and had sex with him and there was an exchange of souls that took place. And even though now you say you are done with him, you have to ask God to release you from any ungodly ties to him. And this is for anyone. Say out loud, "I denounce the spirit of so-and-so and I release them in Jesus' name. And you gotta do that every day until the very thought of that person does not cause your womb to leap; it doesn't cause you to have a reaction to them. I've been there so I'm not judging you. I was involved with a married man and I loved him. This is for anyone that you are involved with that does not belong to you; you have to let them go from your mind and spirit. You get rid of stuff. Clothing, shoes, jewelry, pictures and emails and all of that. Don't pay him back by talking to his wife. Don't expose anybody. Just ask God to take this from me, get him out of me. And do it as often as you think of him and as long as you have a reaction to the thought of him. "God get him out of me. Get him out."

The following is a list of questions for you to ask yourself while you wait for your spouse. They can help you prepare to receive your godly spouse. If you are already married, take some time with your spouse to answer these questions as honestly as you can. Truthful answers can improve and strengthen your relationship. They are not designed to be answered easily or quickly. They should stir up thoughts about areas where you may still be holding on to the past. If you are answering them with your husband, as you go through the questions, be sensitive that some things you may need to share here could be hurtful in the hearing of them. Do your best to communicate without harm or intention to pay back a suffered wrong.

1. Can I identify when I was happiest in my life? What was happening then that made me feel such happiness? Is any of that still happening for me now?

2. Are there areas of my life that I intentionally withhold from my boyfriend/partner/husband? What are they and what makes me intentionally keep them from him?

3. What about intimacy scares me?

4. Can I love unconditionally? Can I love me just the way I am? Can I love someone else just the way they are?

5. Are there unspoken deal-breakers for me in relationships? If so what are they?

6. Are there things that I will not compromise on?

7. What does "love" mean to me? What does being "in love" mean?

8. Do I feel connected to my partner? Is there anything that would make me feel more connected?

9. What concerns me most about life? What am I most afraid of?

10. What do I want my life to look like? Do I feel that I am moving in that direction? If not, what needs to be different?

11. When I think about marriage, what do I expect it to be like? Is that what's happening in my marriage now?

12. Is there anything that I feel unfulfilled about in my life? Is there a way to feel more fulfilled?

13. Is my relationship satisfying to me? What would I like to be better? What would I just like to be different?

14. Are there times when I don't feel respected in my relationship? If so, when is that?

15. What makes me angry?

16. How do I handle my anger?

17. Am I living where I want to live? Am I living the way I want to live?

18. What brings me joy?

19. What are my challenges to intimacy? How to do I deal with them?

20. What do I think are the husband's responsibilities?

21. What do I think are the wife's responsibilities?

22. How would I want to address chores and daily living needs like dinner preparation and cooking, grocery shopping, oil changes for the car or cars, etc.

23. How do I think money should be handled in the family? By whom and how?

24. Is there a "Breadwinner?" if so, who is it?

25. How do I need to be shown love? "I feel loved when _____."

26. How do I want to include friends in my relationship? How do they fit?

27. What do I want to have in common with my husband?

28. In my relationships, do I usually give more than I receive? Is that okay? What do I need to do to change that? Are my relationships one-sided with me giving more than I receive?

29. Are my needs being met in my relationship? If not which are not? Can they be? How?

30. Have I sought God about my relationship or have I been doing what I want to do?

31. Have I prayed for my husband? (even if he hasn't come yet)

32. Do I feel closer to God because of this relationship? Does it make me want to be closer to God?

33. Does this relationship encourage my growth in Christ?

34. Are there issues in my relationship that need to be addressed before I feel comfortable moving forward?

35. Do I have unfinished business from my past that has to be addressed before I feel I can move forward?

36. Am I staying in this relationship to rescue my friend? Am I playing caretaker?

37. Am I staying in this relationship because I don't want to hurt my friend's feelings?

38. Why do I want to get married?

39. Could I be just as happy if I stayed single?

40. Have I ever been abused? Physically, sexually, emotionally, or verbally? Who did I share it with? What was their response? What do I need now?

41. How do I make decisions?

42. What would I be willing to give up to have a successful, happy marriage?

43. What makes me feel safe?

44. Who is responsible for my failed relationships? Me? Or them? Or both of us?

45. Do I feel like I have to change for this relationship to work?

46. Do I have to win arguments? What happens if I lose?

47. Are there red flags that I'm ignoring? Am I willing to hear from wise counsel about any red flags? (Addictions, unfaithfulness, history of being an abuser or of being abused, different spiritual beliefs, conflict and aggression, poor communication, etc.)

48. Do I have secrets?

49. Are we friends first, then spouses? If not, how can we build a stronger friendship?

50. How much do I trust my husband? How can we build more trust, stronger trust?

There is a story that I want to share with you. I need to share with you. It's so important because it really speaks to the relationship that God wants for us and I can't think of a better example.

Throughout this book I've been talking about being the godly wife to your godly husband. I've told you to how important it is to keep your voice and how critical it is to join with your husband as your partner and your friend. I've told you that it is impossible to be a wife without knowing who you are and celebrating your uniqueness in God. I've shared the difference between being a wife and being a wifey. I've talked about not being a side-chick and not emasculating your man.

Now I want to talk about what is available to you in being a godly wife. What's the payoff? Why bother doing all this work? Why seek to have a godly husband in the first place?

A godly husband is your covering. He is the keeper of your heart. He is the buffer between you and everything else, including your past. He is your leader and your soulmate. A godly husband is a natural representation of God in the family. He is to lead with compassion being trustworthy, consistent, available and accessible. He is to serve his family as a leader and he is to lead his family to righteousness. The godly husband is known as a Servant Leader. He is humble before God and strong through God in the stand for his family. He seeks God for direction and stands on scripture as the revealed Truth.

The reality is that no husband leads because he is worthy to lead. The truth is that no one is really sufficient to so great a task. There are at least a million ways we fall short. He knows it. He is aware of it every day. And yet a godly husband doesn't walk away or faint under the weight of it. He re-focuses on what God requires of him. He trusts God and believes that whatever God has brought him to He has also prepared him to receive great success in. Where he feels weak and ill-prepared, he turns to God for guidance and assurance.

A godly husband is not intimidated by his wife's success and accomplishment. He knows that she is not only a reflection of the God who dwells within her, but she represents him as well. They are a partnership. Remember the virtuous woman in Proverbs 31? Remember how her husband regarded her? There was no competition between them. He respected and honored her. He even admired her. While the husband is the leader and head of the family, he is secure enough in himself that he can support his wife in the use of her gifts, talents, skills and abilities without his masculinity being threatened. It is society that has created an unnecessary competition between the gender roles. "Wife" does not mean helpless, sitting at home, waiting for her man to arrive and take care of her. According to scripture, it sounds to me like they are doing well enough between them that there are servants in the home to help maintain it. It seems to me that both the godly wife and husband are skilled in delegation and time and resource management. Where neither of them relinquishes the intimate responsibilities of the home and family, only those where their energy and personal attention are not a necessity.

Your husband has stewardship over the family and ultimate responsibility before God for his family. In importance, he is to place you above himself and below God. I know you've heard it before, but scripture says that the husband is to love his wife, you, as Christ loves the church. What does that mean exactly? It means that he is to love you selflessly. He is to regard you as precious and valuable. He is to love you more than his own life. Your husband is to lead with the mind of Christ, always seeking God's wisdom and perfect will. He prays over and for you and is a good father to your children.

Your husband works to be a good communicator for the sake of the relationship. He makes an effort to hear your heart and to understand without judgment. He seeks first to understand, then to be understood. He makes every attempt to hear with the heart of compassion with an intention to instigate peace. He also recognizes the challenge that it may be for him to express himself clearly. He acknowledges and surrenders to the communication process. And with your loving understanding and patience, his communication skills improve and so do yours.

In the same way that you spend time alone with God, so does your husband. He has a lot of responsibility towards his family and he seeks first God's kingdom and righteousness. He acknowledges God in all of his ways so that God will direct his paths and add success to his footsteps. He keeps God first above all else.

God's plan for your marriage is to create a union of souls that honor Him with their all. Your husband is the catalyst for all of that. He leads you in prayer as well as allows you to stand for him in his weakness. Because he loves and follows God so closely, he can be vulnerable with you as his partner and the lover of his soul.

Your husband is to be a visionary for your family. There should be a core desire to move forward and upward. He should be the depository for new, witty, God-given ideas. He is not satisfied with mediocrity but seeks greater in God. He holds the vision for who your family is to be in the community and the kingdom.

Your husband is to be the protector of his family. Now let me be clear. I'm not talking about taking nobody down in the alley. He should not have to be an Ultimate Fighting

Champion to have your respect and appreciation. Sure it feels great to know your man can throw down if need be. But protection also means something a bit more subtle.

Imagine this situation…in the division of labor in the household, you took on the laundry. Given the way the week went, the laundry didn't get done. Now there are several loads to do and unless they get done, you and your husband will have nothing to wear for the week. It's Sunday night. Because the laundry room in your apartment closes at 10:00 you now have to go to the neighborhood laundromat. No other choice to get it done. You probably won't be done with all the laundry until 1:00 or so in the morning. What should your husband do? He should protect you and he has several options to make that happen. He can go with you. He can go for you. Or you can make some other arrangements together to get the laundry done and figure out what to wear until it happens. By no means should he allow you to go alone to a neighborhood laundromat in the middle of the night. Got that? See how that is an element of protection? Wouldn't you feel valued and highly regarded under those circumstances? This is who your husband is as protector. There may also be times when he has to be a stand for you to protect you from emotional and spiritual attack as well.

The amazing part is who your husband becomes to you. He is your soulmate. He is your best friend. He is able to touch places in you that no one else on earth can. He is able to stand for you and protect you from the world.

This is who my husband became for me, and more. I could never have imagined the love we would have and the trust that would build between us. My husband isn't perfect but he is perfect for me. We continue to grow in love and respect for each other, finding new depths of connection that just amaze and astound me. He is an amazing man and an amazing man of God. I watch him continue to grow in the Lord. He leads our family steadfastly and with certainty. He supports me in every way. He encourages me in my spirit and soul. He stands for my best and my success. He's confident in who I am and I can be authentically, unapologetically who God created me to be.

We've been through a lot together. My Shaun helped me be with my past, and all that I had been through, I could share with him. There was a turning point early on in our relationship that speaks to what it's like to be with a godly husband.

When you and I started this journey together, I shared with you my story. In my story, I told you that I left Atlanta, Georgia after me and my ex got divorced. I drove all the way from Atlanta with a box of tissues, my gospel CD and just enough money to get me home. I also had "The Box." "The Box" has come to symbolize my journey. It represents all that I have been through. It represents the point of no return for me. "The Box" is my surrender to Shaun Collins as my husband and my choice. Here's my story:

It was the day before my wedding to Shaun. I was cleaning out my old closet at my mother and father's house. Deep in the back of the closet, this box was covered with clothes and shoes and other boxes. It had been there for years. Out of sight out of mind, though somewhere in the back of my mind, just under the surface of consciousness, I knew it was there. And I knew it was good for me to go through some of the things in this closet because Shaun and I were moving into our apartment. As I took the items off of this larger box, I realized what that box was…and I paused…and I froze. It had been so long since I had seen that box. So long since I had thought of that box and all that it contained. All of the memories of what I went through and all of the things I remembered, that I had collected, were in that box and came flooding back to me. Everything was in there – postcards, letters, cards, memorabilia, pictures, jewelry, knickknacks, teddy bears, even lingerie – was all in that box. So I got the box out of the closet and was holding it tightly. The box was very, very heavy.

I made it to the top of the stairs and I called
Shaun to me from the family room. He met me at the
bottom of the stairs, looking up at me. I told him quietly
that I needed to tell him something. He was silent
waiting for me to continue. I said, "Shaun. This box.
I've got to get rid of it." He asked me what was in the
box and I told him it had "some things from my past."
And I put my head down. He asked me what I was
going to do with it. And I said, "I have to get rid of it
because I can't marry you tomorrow knowing what's in
this box." And I began to cry as I started down the
stairs. At the same time he started up the stairs and met
me halfway. And again the box was heavy but I was
holding it as if I could carry the weight by myself. As I
neared him, Shaun extended his hands toward me as if
to take the box from me. I was holding the box out but
at the same time I didn't want to let the box go. I knew
when I let the box go I was completely letting go of all
of my past. My past with my ex-husband, the past with
all the things that I've gone through. As if he could
sense my struggle, Shaun so gently and so sweetly,
rubbed my hand and said, "It's okay, babe, it's okay.
I'll get rid of it for you." And the tears began to flow
even harder from my eyes. And my heart began to race.
And he took the box from my hands and he told me,

"You'll never see this again." When I heard that, I thought, okay, we're gonna get rid of this box together. Then he turned, looked back at me and said, "I'm gonna get rid of the box." Then he walked out of the front door. I don't know to this day what he did with that box. I don't know if he burned it. I don't know if he threw it in the river. I don't know if he dumped it in the trash. All I know is I saw my then-fiancé take something from me that was so heavy I could hardly bear the weight of it. After years of hiding under the shame of that box and all that it meant, he looked me in the eyes and told me I'd never see this box again and I didn't have to worry about it. I knew then that no matter what I was going to go through with Shaun or what we'd have to face, he was my soulmate. He made me feel so safe. He didn't make me feel like I was crazy or like something was wrong with me for holding on to something for so many years and still having the emotional ties to it. He rescued me. Shaun instantly became my hero. I thought of what Jesus said in His Word, to cast your cares upon Me because I care for you. I'm a burden-bearer. I'm a heavy load-sharer. I nailed your sins and sickness and your burdens and all of that to the cross.

I watched my God-given husband walk away with all of my shame, all of my grief, all of my sorrow, all of my rejection, and all of my self-hatred in that box. And I trusted him. And I loved him even more.

And I finally let it all go.

God healed me emotionally from heartbreak and rejection and physically from sickness and disease.

The following information is very powerful. Here are the scriptures I read, the words I said, and the very practical things I did daily for MY healing. I encourage you to try them.

Every day until I actually felt a release, I practiced forgiving my ex-husband and other men. It wasn't easy, but it was necessary. I could no longer be the victim! I wanted to love again, so being bitter and angry was not an option. I spoke the Word of God over myself.

For Emotional Healing, these are the things I said:

1) I forgive "_____" until I don't feel the urge or pull to make him/them feel what I endured. Matthew 18:21-22 King James Version: "[21]Then came Peter to him, and said, Lord, how oft shall my brother sin against me, and I forgive him? Till seven times? [22]Jesus saith unto him, I say not unto thee, until seven times, but, until seventy times seven."

2) I release myself from all anger and fear. God you have NOT given me a spirit of fear! You've given me Power, Love, and sound mind! 2 Timothy 1:7: "For God hath not given us the spirit of fear, but of

power, and of love, and of a sound mind." I am not weak; I am strong!

3) I forgive myself. My life doesn't end after divorce! I will love again! I will use this as a lesson on what not to do or accept when or if I marry again.

4) I am a whole woman. Not half, not a quarter, but a complete, whole woman. There is nothing broken about me or within me.

5) I will not experience this kind of loss again. God is restoring the years now. Joel 2:25: "And I will restore to you the years that the locusts hath eaten, the cankerworm, and the caterpillar, and the palmerworm, my great army which I sent among you."

6) I will love again with no limits and let someone love me unconditionally. I refuse to be in the way of the blessings God is sending me.

For Emotional Healing, these are the things I did:

1) Have an erase ceremony (old texts, emails, social media contacts, direct messages, pictures, voicemails and videos etc.) – **Block:** No more access, no more interference. **Delete:** Get it out my face. I don't need to be reminded of the thing that hurt until I was healed and overcame the pain of

what I went through. **Trash:** Go a step above delete! Get rid of it for good. With delete you can still recover the info, but when you "trash" it, it's gone for good!

2) Be around positive people. Intentionally have fun and laugh. Laughter is like medicine. According to Proverbs 17:22, "A merry heart doeth good [like] a medicine, but a broken spirit drieth the bones." Do not entertain negative people and their opinions.

3) Pray and worship daily; fast and consecrate by turning away my plate, turning off the phone, the television, and social media. Make time for God and come away from the noise and chatter for a while.

4) Read the Bible and books that revive and refresh the spirit. Listen to powerful worship and praise music.

God also healed my body and delivered me from Graves' disease. I had been challenged with that for nearly ten years.

For Physical Healing, these are the things I said:

1) Healing belongs to me! Not sickness and disease. Deuteronomy 7:15: "And the LORD will take away from thee all sickness, and will put none of the evil

diseases of Egypt, which thou knowest, upon thee, but will lay them upon all that hate thee."

2) I am healed by the Word of God. Isaiah 53:5: "But he was wounded for our transgressions, he was bruised for our iniquities: the chastisement of our peace was upon him; and with his stripes we are healed."

3) My body is the temple of the HOLY GHOST. I know what the facts say but they are not the truth. The truth is I am healed in Jesus' name! I break cycles and generational curses of sickness off my life. I confess with my mouth that my faith has risen up today. Hebrews 11:1: "Now faith is the substance of things hoped for, the evidence of things not seen."

4) No weapon formed against my body or emotions shall be able to prosper! Isaiah 54:17: "No weapon that is formed against thee shall prosper; and every tongue that shall rise against thee in judgment thou shalt condemn. This is the heritage of the servants of the LORD, and their righteousness is of me, saith the LORD."

5) I will trust the Lord even in sickness! He wants me to be well. 3 John 1:2: "Beloved, I wish above all

things that thou mayest prosper and be in health, even as thy soul prospereth."

For Physical Healing, these are the things I did:

1) I took the medication prescribed! I prayed over it and took it until I felt a release not to take it anymore.

2) I obeyed God and fasted for 22 days. I did a dry fast, a water fast, and then a fruit and veggie regimen. Whatever God said, I did. I was desperate and determined to be healed.

3) I walked and exercised at least 4 times a week.

4) I read the Bible and spoke the scripture.

5) Wash, rinse and repeat until change comes!

Notes

Notes

Gleaming with an abundant amount of gratitude, delivering heart-felt messages with passion, and walking with unshakable conviction, Markita D. Collins is living proof that spirit-driven purpose generates boundless blessings and undeniable success.

Rising CEO Markita D. Collins is a top 100 international live streaming social media influencer who is helping to shape the minds of many as an entrepreneur, recording artist, and anointed mentor. Her rapidly growing empire includes GIRL TALK with KITA, Kita's Kookies and Treats, Kita's Kompany and Imagine Media, LLC.

Collins resides in Pennsylvania with her husband Shaun, their two boys and twin girls.

For booking information regarding speaking and ministering at special events, private consulting or media interviews, please contact Team Kita at: staff@MarkitaDCollins.com. To learn about classes, coaching and other Markita D. Collins resources, visit MarkitaDCollins.com.